D0728867

Madison Walks

Madison
WALKS

Harriet Brown &
Jamie Young

J O N E S
B O O K S
Madison, Wisconsin

Copyright © 2003
Harriet Brown and Jamie Young

Jones Books
309 N. Hillside Terrace
Madison, Wisconsin 53705
www.jonesbooks.com

Library of Congress Cataloging-in-Publication Data

Brown, Harriet, 1958-
    Madison walks / by Harriet Brown and Jamie Young.
        p. cm.
    Includes bibliographical references and index.
    ISBN 0-9721217-4-9 (alk. paper)
        1. Madison (Wis.)—Tours. 2.Walking—Wisconsin—
    Madison—Guidebooks.   I. Young, Jamie. II. Title.

    F589.M13B76 2003
    917.75'8304—dc22

                                    2003019413

Printed in the United States of America

                3 5 7 9 10 8 6 4 2

CONTENTS

ACKNOWLEDGMENTS

We're grateful to the many people who helped with this book one way or another. Thanks goes to Joan Laurion, walking partner extraordinaire, who slogged through the rain time and time again and who was always up for one more walk. Thanks also to Kay Cahill, who let us tag along on her dog park walks even though (or maybe because) we don't have a dog.

Several people were extremely helpful in fact-checking walks and correcting egregious errors of direction and description, especially Jan Coombs and Molly Fifield Murray. Any remaining errors are ours and ours alone.

Thanks to Joan Strasbaugh, who invited us to create this book. Finally, thanks to our daughters, Anna and Soleil, who schlepped along on walks when they would rather have been doing other things, but who managed to have some fun anyway. You're the best!

INTRODUCTION

Almost every day of his adult life, my grandfather went for a walk. Around the block, through a park—it didn't matter where he went, as long as he was walking. He didn't wear hiking boots; he carried no fancy water bottles or knapsacks. He just went. I think his daily walks are part of the reason he lived to be 97. Of course it could have been the cigars…but that's another story.

Walking is both a means to an end—we walk to get somewhere—and an end unto itself. We walk for the sake of walking, exercising both body and mind. When I'm in need of inspiration, a creative kick in the pants, I lace up my sneakers and go, and find the miles eating themselves up while I wrestle my demons. There's solace in the soothing repetition of step after step, in the heady flow of oxygen and ideas.

Other times, I just need a dose of the natural world. And while I enjoy biking and cross-country skiing,

they move me through the landscape too quickly.
Only when I walk do I feel I've experienced a place
fully, feeling the tall grass against my bare legs,
breathing in the powerful scent of chamomile,
tripping over boulders, exploring the side routes.
It's all part of being there—not just getting to a
destination but being present every step of the way,
literally and metaphorically.

Besides, walking is the ultimate independent activity.
While rambling with a friend can be wonderful, it's
just as good solo. You can walk by yourself, any time,
any place. You go exactly where you want to go, on
your own schedule, and get to see the world while
you're at it—not a bad deal.

So I hope you enjoy the walks in this book, which are
some of our favorite rambles in and around Madison.
A couple of caveats apply: Distances are approximate,
and all represent the length of the round-trip. While
we clocked a few of these walks by bike or by car, we
made educated guesses on most. And since pace and
walking style vary from person to person—and since
you may want to spend an hour on something we
cruised through in 10 minutes, or vice versa—walking
times are approximate, too. Where the walk is marked
as a loop, it returns along a different route; if it's not
marked as a loop, you must retrace your steps to the
beginning.

Happy trails!

Harriet Brown

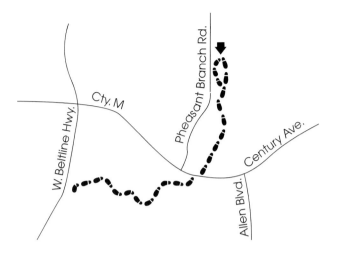

1. Pheasant Branch Creek

The sum of the whole is this: walk and be happy;
walk and be healthy. The best way to lengthen out our days
is to walk steadily and with a purpose.
—Charles Dickens

Off Century Avenue and Pheasant Branch Road, in Middleton

Lower Section

Natural interest

Length: About 2.5 miles; about 1 hour

Loop: No

Terrain: Dirt paths, boardwalk; accessible to wheelchairs and strollers most places.

Note: This walk follows Pheasant Branch Creek and is quite buggy in mosquito season.

This pair of walks isn't in Madison proper but in Middleton, its nearest neighbor to the west. But don't let a little thing like a boundary line keep you from these pleasant perambulations through the Pheasant Branch Conservancy.

Surrounded on three sides by urban development, the conservancy comprises a pleasing variety of terrains, from wetlands to prairie to forest. There's an upper section and a lower section, each with its own distinct character and feeling—a walk for every mood and fancy.

To get there, head west on Century Avenue in Middleton. Turn right at the traffic light at Frank Lloyd Wright Avenue and then right again onto

Pheasant Branch Road. Park in the lot about 0.7 of a mile down the road and start with the lower section of the conservancy. Its half-dozen crossings of Pheasant Branch Creek are especially appealing to children.

The path is wood-chipped and clearly marked, and leads from the parking lot down a slope behind Middleton Hills, a planned community built by local developer Marshall Erdman. The several hundred families who live here like the old-fashioned feeling of the neighborhood and the way shops, offices, and houses cluster to give a small-town feeling to this community within a community.

At the bottom of the hill, turn right and go about a quarter mile to a boardwalk that leads you into the woods. In summer look for the distinctive leaves and bright flowers of jewelweed on either side of the boardwalk. A 90-degree turn takes you over a small wooden bridge—the first of several times you'll cross Pheasant Branch Creek on this walk. One summer afternoon we saw a kingfisher swoop down the creek here, skimming the water, searching for its next meal.

On the other side of the creek, turn right onto a wide, grassy trail that follows the creek upstream. About a quarter of a mile down, take a small side path down to the water. It's a little steep, but there's a reward at the end of the path: a rare patch of jack-in-the-pulpits, with their bright red "jacks" tucked under veined leaves.

Haul yourself up the slope and back onto the main trail, which meanders through the woods. The trail

seems to end at busy Century Avenue, but if you cross Century and look to the right, you'll find another trail, which follows the creek and leads into the next area of the conservancy. Look for raspberry, purple phlox, and the low umbrella-like leaves and tiny inedible fruit of mayapples along the trailsides.

The trail flirts with the creek, veering off in other directions but always returning, following the sound of clear, flowing water. After a short distance, you'll come to the first of several spots where a series of tall, smooth stepping stones crosses the creek. The stones are close together, and children love to hop, skip, and jump across the shallow water. (Keep a close eye on them, though; the stones can be slippery.)

On the other side of the creek, look for the small white flowers of bedstraw. This unusual plant feels sticky because of the little hairs on its stalks and leaves. Pioneers stuffed their mattresses with bedstraw, which doesn't compress the way other plants do. A mattress stuffed with bedstraw is reputed to be softer than a mattress stuffed with grass or other greenery, but we've never tried it.

A short walk brings you to another creek crossing, this one in front of a tiny waterfall. Two more creek crossings follow in short order, each with its own set of stepping stones. After the fourth such crossing the trail crosses Park Street, and once again you enter another part of this section of the conservancy. Go downhill, past two large culverts and into a section of wetlands under restoration. The wooded trail rises and falls gently, still following the creekbed.

Cross the creek one more time on a set of stepping stones that are much bigger than the others. Stairs on your left lead up a steep wooded bank and into the backyard of Middleton High School.

The trail continues a little farther, dead-ending just under the Beltline. There's no loop back to the parking lot, so you have to retrace your steps.

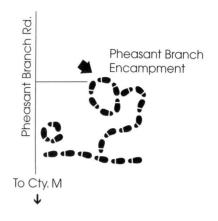

Upper Section
Natural interest, historical interest
Length: 1.5 miles; 30 minutes to 1-1/2 hours
Loop: Yes
Terrain: Grassy trail, dirt path, occasionally steep; not
         recommended for wheelchairs and strollers

The upper section of the Pheasant Branch
Conservancy is best reached by driving a half mile
beyond the lot for the lower section (see page 2).
Turn right just past a mailbox and park in the lot on
the left, near a plaque commemorating Black Hawk's
1832 encampment at Pheasant Branch. Then hike
down the dirt trail that leads away from the parking
lot, through a gate and toward an odd little hill
directly in front of you. This hill was left standing
after the glaciers finished rearranging this part of the
Wisconsin landscape, and it's still one of the highest
elevations in Dane County.

The best time to take this walk is early summer, when you're hungry for the sights and smells of sun and earth and life: tiny grasshoppers whirring up from the ground under your nose, the feeling of sun warming your shoulders, the glint of red on the tail of a hawk soaring high above you. Stroll through a landscape of rolling cornfields and prairie, where the intense green is broken only by shimmering patches of golden yarrow. Tiny yellow chamomile flowers spring up along the dirt path, releasing their sweet, spicy scent—the unmistakable smell of summertime—with every step you take.

Follow the grassy mowed path up to and around the back of the hill. The path gets pretty steep, and you'll need to stop and catch your breath, which gives you a perfect opportunity to admire the view. Ignore the townhouses crowding along one side; the rest of the vista is pastoral and lovely, conjuring images of long, lazy summer days in the country.

Continue up and around the hill, watching for monarch butterflies flitting around stalks of milkweed. Another

five minutes' climbing brings you to the top of the hill. Relax on a bench in the shade of a couple of massive oaks, where a small observation deck looks out over the marsh below. Swallows swoop and dive through the oak canopy. In the distance, Pheasant Branch (*branch* means creek or stream) winds lazily away, like a picture-book representation of a river. The blue glimmer on the horizon is Lake Mendota, gleaming over the trees near the tiny dome of the far-off capitol. This is one of the few spots around Madison where you get this kind of altitude, and it's well worth the effort of getting here.

When you're ready to move on, head back to the trail and bear left onto a wooded path that loops around the top of the hill and quickly rejoins the main trail. Turn left and head back down along the trail you hiked up on.

Bear left at the next fork, right at the fork after that, and then left onto another path that heads downhill along a fenceline that brings you to a sunny observation platform overlooking the Pheasant Branch Springs. You may catch a flash of gold in the trees across the creek, where magnolia warblers can be spotted in May and June. But the real show is down in the shallow water, where the creekbed appears to be boiling. It's a startling sight, partly because the water is so clear: bubbles of sand and water tumble continuously to the surface, as if a sea serpent deep below the sand were lashing its tail. These springs and another set nearby pump more than 2.6 million gallons of water a day into the marsh and, eventually, Lake Mendota.

Retrace your steps up along the fenceline. At the top, head left toward the main trail, and you'll be back at the parking lot within 10 minutes.

RESOURCES

- www.erdman.com/mhills
  Website of Middleton Hills.

- www.pheasantbranch.org
  Website of the Friends of Pheasant Branch, a group of community members who provide stewardship and volunteer labor to maintain the Pheasant Branch Conservancy.

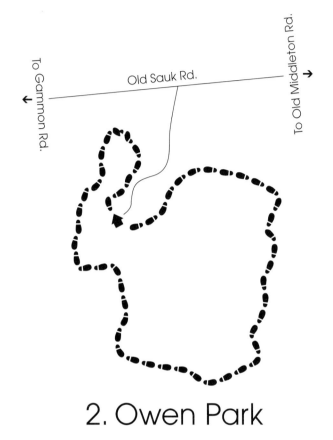

2. Owen Park

An early-morning walk is a blessing for the whole day.
—Henry David Thoreau

6021 Old Sauk Road

Natural interest
Length: Varies
Loop: Yes
Terrain: Hilly; dirt and grass trails; not recommended
         for strollers or wheelchairs

Be thankful for glaciers. Thousands of years ago they slid over this part of southcentral Wisconsin and made the landscape interesting, creating high ridges, shallow valleys, dips, and other topographic features.

The particular feature that makes up most of Owen Park is what geologists call a recessional moraine, a kind of hiccup marking the spot where a glacier receded before moving southward again. The glacier left behind some of the debris it carried in its wake, enough to make a nice little bump in an otherwise flat landscape.

You can climb this bump when you walk the trails at Owen Park, enjoying every inch of altitude. And if you're out early on a clear morning, you can also see a lovely sunrise.

Owen Park was once a farm belonging to Edward T. Owen, a professor of French at the University of Wisconsin in the late nineteenth century. Like other conservation parks, Owen Park was acquired by the city to restore native plant and animal communities so that people could enjoy and learn about them. It's not as showy as Madison's waterfront parks; nor is it as big and wild as, say, the area around Frautschi Point. But there's something very pleasing about its laid-back accessibility.

There are two sets of trails here, an upper and a lower. Each set contains many smaller, interconnected paths that wind around and together and, eventually, bring you back to your starting place. If you're out at dawn, start with the lower set, which gives the best view of the rising sun.

Begin at the far end of the parking lot, where a map is posted by a trailhead. Of the three trails before you, take the one that's farthest to the right, which will lead you to a 20-minute walk around the largest possible loop. This wide grassy trail skirts the edge of a prairie alight with purple coneflowers and small sunflowers in summer. Keep heading downhill as prairie gives way to oak savanna.

Massive oak trees rise up here and there, their twisted limbs and magnificent crowns like sculptures. The tall prairie grasses all bend in the same direction, with the prevailing winds, giving this section of the park the look of an African savanna. You half expect a lion to rise silkily out of the grass and pad away.

Bear right at a fork, staying to the perimeter of the savanna. Follow the grassy path past a magnificent stand of staghorn sumac trees. Some people consider the sumac a nuisance tree, a weedy volunteer that gets in the way of the main event, but we've always loved their expressive limbs and violently colored "horns," which can be used to make wine.

Near the bottom of the hill, stop to admire a sprawling example of the mighty oak. This specimen extends its branches over the path, shading a wide area. Narrower side paths loop off the main trail throughout this part of the walk, and occasional benches provide a restful, invigorating view of the prairie and savanna.

Around the far side of the savanna, the path starts to rise steeply. Watch for monarch butterflies in summer, sipping their way homeward. About halfway up the hill, bear left onto a wide grassy trail that cuts across a grassy section. From here you have the best chance of seeing the sun streak the sky orange and gold as it climbs the horizon. Follow this path back up the hill to the parking lot.

The upper set of trails are narrower, and take you through woods that change from sunny to shady and back again a dozen times. Start at the near end of the parking lot, with the trail that leads uphill past a small maintenance building. Bear right a short way up the

trail at the fork, and keep winding your way up and around the moraine. You can't get lost, since the trails loop around and across, intersecting one another at various points around the hillside.

Owen Park is home to many kinds of birds, and these upper trails are favored by birdwatchers. You almost can't help catching sight of cardinals, chickadees, and other common birds. Listen for woodpeckers tapping their lightning-fast messages into the trees. On one winter walk we saw an owl high in a hemlock tree. It was easily twice the size of any owl we had ever seen, and its fierce beauty was astonishing.

In spring, the dusty lavender stems of raspberry bushes curve up from the ground beside the trail like exotic sculptures. In summer, jewelweed springs up in abundance. Rest for a moment on a bench overlooking a glade full of ferns, their feathery heads nodding gently in the wind. A half-dozen or so trails wind in and out of woods, leading you from sun to shade and back again.

When you're ready to go back, just head downhill, and you'll quickly find your way along one of the interlocking paths to the parking lot.

Extend the Walk: One of the appeals of living in
Madison is the sheer number of parks within and just
outside the city limits. Each park has its own distinct
character. Two others to explore and enjoy are Hoyt
Park, on the near west side, and Warner Park to the
northeast. Both have well-marked trails and maps
posted to guide you along their paths.

RESOURCES

- madconservation.tripod.com
  A website devoted to Madison's conservation parks.

- www.ci.madison.wi.us/parks
  The city of Madison's home page for parks, with links to
  activities, park shelters, calendars, volunteer opportunities,
  and other useful information about local parks.

- www.rockvillemama.com/dane/owenedwardt.txt
  This site, part of the Wisconsin Biographies Project,
  features biographies of Edward T. Owen and other eminent
  Madisonians.

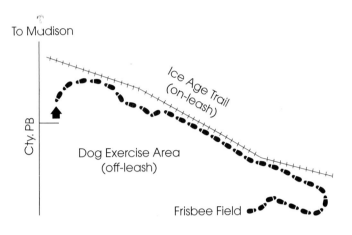

To Madison

Ice Age Trail
(on-leash)

Cty. PB

Dog Exercise Area
(off-leash)

Frisbee Field

3. Prairie Moraine Park—the Dog Park

My grandmother started walking five miles a day when she was 60. She's 93 today and we don't know where the hell she is.—Ellen DeGeneres

County Highway PB, near Verona

Natural interest

Length: Anywhere between a quarter mile and several miles; as much or as little time as you want

Loop: Yes

Terrain: Mildly hilly; well-marked dirt trails (but watch out for doggy calling cards); not recommended for strollers or wheelchairs

Big dogs. Little dogs. Black dogs and white dogs. Dogs going up and dogs coming down. Dogs going away in cars. Dogs wearing party hats.

OK, you probably won't see party hats, but the rest of the spectrum of canine behavior is yours to observe and enjoy at Prairie Moraine Park, otherwise known as the dog park. Dane County actually has nine parks where dogs are allowed to romp off-leash, and four of those are in Madison: Brittingham, Quann, Sycamore, and Warner parks. Each park has its loyal followers, who prefers it to all others. Our favorite is Prairie Moraine.

To get to the park, take Highway 18/151 to exit 79, turn left at Highway PB, and go a mile or two until you see the sign for Prairie Moraine Park. Park in the lot on your left and slip in through the gate, remembering to close it behind you so off-leash dogs don't escape.

If you have even a tiny spark of canine appreciation in your heart, you will thrill to the sight of dogs of every

size, breed, and degree of furriness. Even if you aren't a dog owner (and we're not), it's worth driving a little way out of town for a brisk early-morning stroll here, because the dog park is one of the best people-watching spots around. Forget State Street or the campus—for checking out human behavior, you can't beat the dog park on Sunday morning.

The dog-watching's pretty good, too. After a visit or two you notice that dogs seem to visit the park in cycles. One week every other dog you see is a Doberman; the next, dachshunds are de rigueur. And why is it that some dogs really, really do look like their people?

There's an etiquette and a rhythm to a dog park visit. Bring a water bottle and a bowl, and leave them on one of the picnic tables just inside the gate; they'll come in handy later. (The human accessory du jour is a blue plastic bag swinging jauntily from one hand, radiating the unmistakable aroma of fresh you-know-what.) Then snap off your dog's leash and head uphill on one of the park's well-marked and wood-chipped trails.

A dog alone is only half a dog, so the first thing dogs do (besides *that*) is head for the other dogs. They

rarely bowl over bystanders, but you never know if your knees can withstand 85 pounds of golden retriever until you've experienced it. Some of these extemporaneous packs are made up of canine buddies deep in the midst of joyous reunions. Others are newfound friends, their noses deep in one another's hindquarters. They roll. They sniff. They bond.

What with packs of racing canines, it can be hard to stick to a prescribed walking trail. So just follow your dog (or someone else's) uphill, where eventually you will come to two important landmarks: a fragrant mountain of wood chips, and a vertical high-voltage tower. From there all trails lead downhill and, eventually, back to the parking lot.

The terrain is suitable for an aerobic stroll: a wide expanse of rolling glacial hills. There's no particular route, just miles of crisscrossing dirt trails that loop and wind and follow the topography. Some of the trails weave through what looks like an old Christmas tree farm gone wild. In spots you have to squeeze through narrow passages between trees.

The dogs don't mind. They gallop through chest-high grasses and pelt through squat overgrown evergreens, their tongues hanging out, dog slobber flying.

Just for Fun

Names we've heard at the dog park:
Chelvis, Molly, Skip, Macker, Randolph, Fiona,
Gunnar, Bud, Siri, Katie, Beauregard, Maude,
Maxwell, Cody, Mattie. You know you've got a
trendy name (for your child or your pet) when
you hear it echoing off the hills at Prairie
Moraine.

Breeds we've seen:
Bedlington terrier, Llewelyn setter, bloodhound,
collie, beagle, basset hound, chocolate lab,
vizsla, malamute, shepherd, Lhasa apso,
standard poodle, papillon, Doberman,
English springer spaniel, boxer, and, of course,
Heinz 57.

Most aptly named dog we've met:
Calamity, a bloodhound

They are joyful and exuberant and enthusiastic.
They are dogs.

Back at the foot of the hill, while your dog is slurping
water out of a plastic bowl, amuse yourself by reading
the notices posted on a bulletin board just inside the

gate. There you can find groomers, obedience classes, and all manner of canine-connected things for sale. The last and final trick of the walk is to releash your dog. This should be easy, since a romp at the park will tire even the most enthusiastic dog. But many a furry quadruped has slipped out the gate without a leash. Fortunately the humans at the dog park are usually happy to reach out and grab someone else's collar.

RESOURCES

- www.dogpark.f2s.com
  The website for the Prairie Moraine Dog Park, including news, a discussion group, photos, lost and found, and volunteer opportunities

Seminole Hwy.

Visitor Center

Entrance to park

W. Beltline Hwy.

4. The Arboretum—North

*And I walking out into all of this with nowhere to go and no
task undertaken but to turn the pages of this beautiful
world over and over in the world of my mind.*
—Mary Oliver

1207 Seminole Highway

Natural interest
Length: About 2 miles; 30 minutes to 1 hour
Loop: Yes
Terrain: Easy, relatively flat; some sections (especially
        Wingra Woods) not recommended for
        wheelchairs and strollers

New Yorkers have the New York Botanical Garden.
Madisonians have the Arboretum. Their missions are
different, but the result is the same: a place where city
folk can experience Nature (with a capital N).
Madisonians have a lot less city to get away from than
New Yorkers, but it's the principle of the thing.

Back in the 1920s, this green space was the intended
site of a new housing development that was to be dug
out of the marshland, complete with canals and
lagoons—the Venice of the Midwest. But a
combination of swampy land, inadequate roads, and
the Depression killed the project. The developers
abandoned their half-built houses and roads, the land
was sold for the Arboretum, and the whole thing
passed into history as the Lost City.

The Arboretum itself was dedicated in June 1934, an
experiment designed to reconstruct "a sample of what
Dane County looked like when our ancestors arrived
here during the 1840s," as naturalist Aldo Leopold put

it. No one knows whether the experiment succeeded, of course, since none of us were alive in 1840. Over the years, the Arboretum has expanded to its present 1,280 acres and 20 miles of trails, encompassing a range of landscapes, from prairie and wetland to conifer forest and garden.

The entrance to the Arboretum is off Seminole Highway. Follow the road in for about half a mile and park. Then begin your walk behind the renovated Visitor Center, at the circular terrace garden. Head north into the Longenecker Gardens, 60 acres of dazzling horticultural plantings. On peak weekend days in spring, a steady stream of visitors flows through these gardens, admiring the strange beauty of magnolias, their pink and white flowers bursting out of dead-looking branches.

The gardens are full of wonderful plantings: azaleas, flowering crabapple, hawthorns older than we are. The most spectacular flowering takes place in May, when more than 200 species of lilacs burst into fragrant bloom. The first lilacs here were planted around 1935, and they're still very popular; in fact, there are people who come to the Arboretum only once a year, to experience the glory of the lilacs in bloom.

Continue north, through an area planted with all manner of oaks—scarlet, sawtooth, columnar, chestnut. Follow the fenceline through the oak and ash, toward a field of short bushy pines and taller ones, their long needles gracefully depending from their branches. Pines give way to spruce, and a well-placed bench offers a view of the lawn leading back to the Visitor Center.

Keep walking uphill through juniper and other conifers. At the crest of the hill, find the break in the fence to your left and slip through, past the bike rack, across the road and into a small parking lot. Follow the trail at the west end of the parking lot, leading off to the left through a sweet-smelling forest of pine. After a long winter, this pleasant woodland trail is like water to a parched throat, alive with green growing things.

Turn right as the trail curves to the right, away from the road, and head downhill. In early spring patches of brilliant white bloodroot, violets, and wild geranium light up the woods. At another T a short way down the trail, turn right again. The trail becomes slightly wider here as it makes its way through this part of Lake Wingra's watershed. You quickly arrive at Big Spring, once a spring to reckon with but now—like the rest of Lake Wingra's water table—a shadow of its original glory. From the small

flagstoned overlook, you can see the humble
beginnings of Lake Wingra.

Rest your feet on the bench for a while. When you're
ready, continue along the original path. This part of
the Arboretum has no spectacular features, but if you
pay attention, you'll observe plenty of subtle beauty:
light slanting through a cluster of trees, a
woodpecker's syncopated knocking.

Continue along the trail until you reach marker K4.
Turn right (south) and walk up a slight incline,
through hemlock and yellow birch. Wingra Woods, a
restored northern Wisconsin forest planted with
hemlock, sugar maple, birch, and other species, has
an open, sunlit feeling and plenty of gentle dips and
rises that give away its glacial past. One afternoon
here we met a mounted policewoman, one of seven
mounted officers who patrol the county. She and her
horse were enjoying a ramble through the woods just
like those of us on foot.

Follow the trail across the road and into Gallistel
Woods, one of the best-known sections of the
Arboretum. Stay on the path as it intersects a cross-
country ski trail. This section of the woods is airy and
pleasant—perfect for a Sunday walk.

When you reach a small stone building on your right,
turn left and follow the sign toward the Teal Pond
Wetlands. A short boardwalk takes you across a
marshy area and ends in a small gazebo with benches,
where you can sit and observe the quiet beauty of a
Wisconsin wetland. (This part of the walk is best done

in early spring or after a hard frost, unless you're one of the lucky few who aren't bothered by mosquitoes.)

Retrace your steps along the boardwalk, back to the trail crossing at the stone building. Turn left and continue up the trail, through the Southern Wisconsin Maple Forest Restoration. At a T, turn right and then right again to find yourself back in the Longenecker Gardens, well on your way back to the Visitor Center.

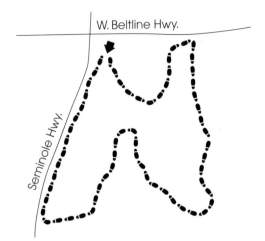

W. Beltline Hwy.

Seminole Hwy.

5. The Arboretum— South

Methinks that the moment my legs begin to move, my thoughts begin to flow.—Henry David Thoreau

Off Seminole Highway and the Beltline

Natural interest

Length: About 2.5 miles, or 1 hour

Loop: Yes

Terrain: For the most part, easy flat trails and/or easy woodland paths; can be very muddy in spring and into summer.

Note: Long pants are advisable for the prairie section.

I strolled the Arboretum for years before I realized there was another section of land south of the Beltline.

The Grady Tract, as it's called, doesn't have the spectacular flowering trees and plantings of its northern counterpart. But over the last few years, the understated beauty of these woods has made this one of our favorite Madison walks.

For the spatially challenged, this walk has one big advantage: wooden markers with coordinates posted at strategic locations along the trail. These markers (unlike markers on other trails we've walked) actually match up with the markers on the map. They make excellent landmarks and will help even the least woods-wise walker navigate with confidence.

This walk has one significant disadvantage, too: it's close to several big roads, so the sound of speeding cars is always with you. With a little concentration, though, you can learn to block out the noise.

Park in the tiny lot at the corner of Seminole Highway and the Beltline and take one of the maps at the

entrance to the Arboretum. In summer, trail markers can be overgrown or hidden, and a map helps keep you oriented.

Squeeze through the fence opening and follow the trail that bears right, which leads into a wooded area. About 75 yards down the trail, bear right onto another trail. See if you can spot wild columbine.

At a grassy fork, bear right. If you're here in May, look deep in the shrubby trailside growth for an occasional tree ablaze with white blossoms—old apple trees still putting out their radiant spring flowers.

After about a quarter mile, the trail widens and turns away from the road. Look for cherry, swamp oak, maple, and sumac beside the trail. This is one of the muddiest, swampiest sections of the walk; it's possible to slog through in sneakers (we did), but hiking boots make for a drier passage.

From here you can see a piece of the Capital City Bike Trail. You can also see, on a hillside to the right, a controversial housing development that was built a

couple of years ago. Runoff from this development has flooded parts of the Grady Tract.

At marker X8, turn left and head deeper into the woods. On one of our spring walks, this section of trail was in fact underwater, but a short boardwalk circumvents the worst of the wet part and eventually leads you back onto dry land. In the meantime, the underwater section is eerily, unusually beautiful. Spring frogs sing a continuous ratcheting melody that sounds like a crowd of children twirling noisemakers. You might be deep in a Louisiana swamp, gliding through a world half water and half land.

Once the trail dries, it runs along a wetland and comes out at a section of prairie that's being restored to oak savanna. Turn right at marker X3, by the stone honoring Arboretum ecologist Virginia Kline, who retired in 1996.

One of the nicest things about this walk is its relative seclusion. On a brilliant afternoon in May we saw only a handful of other hikers, each lost in his or her contemplation of the natural world. We did spot a number of nonhuman denizens, including a red-tailed hawk, a woodpecker, and a pair of turkeys. The male turkey fanned his colorful tail feathers, looking like a Thanksgiving centerpiece. The female picked her way through the leafy grass, unconcerned and seemingly unaware. Eventually she wandered off, leaving the male to meekly fold his tail and follow.

Follow the trail downhill to marker Z1, and turn right onto a small path that leads you into the heart of Greene Prairie. The path (which alternates with boardwalk) is narrow and overgrown; at times you feel you're swimming through a sea of tall grasses and flowers. At the height of summer the path is hidden beneath the profusion of growing things, and you may have to feel for it with your feet.

Created by botanist Henry Greene over a period of 15 years in the 1940s and '50s, Greene Prairie is widely regarded as one of the best examples of restored prairie in the world. Sadly, it, too, is compromised by nearby housing developments. Runoff from the developments creates unnaturally wet conditions on the prairie and carries the seeds of an invasive species called reed canary grass, which is threatening to outcompete the butterfly weed, phlox, prairie dock, lady's slipper, and other species of prairie plants.

So walk this wild path while you can. Look out over the living, breathing prairie and imagine what this corner of the world looked like 500 years ago. A lot like this, no doubt. On a hot summer day, dark butterflies flutter in the sun, lighting on tall stalks of delicate lavender blooms, bright yellow flowers, and whiplike green stems.

Emerge from the prairie at marker Z5 and turn left onto a sandy trail. At marker Z4, bear left, and then bear right at marker Y8, admiring the plentiful small hills in this part of the Arboretum landscape. Plunge straight through a four-way trail intersection and continue on. Coming around the curve here one day we saw a large doe, her head down and tail switching. She looked up and stared, and we stared back. Then she loped into the shrubby woods. When we approached, we saw the heart-shaped marks of her hooves dug into the sandy trailside.

You're close to the Beltline here. In fact, if you keep heading straight on this section of trail, you'll walk under the Beltline and into the main part of the Arboretum. Bear left instead, into an area of tall, stately pines, and walk quietly. You just might come face to face with a couple of leggy yearling deer, and have the chance to watch them leap gracefully away. Breathe deep as you go, because the trail is covered with pine needles and smells deliciously of evergreen and fresh air.

After a slight uphill section, you'll come out at marker U3 onto a gravelly trail. The intersection is marked by a stand of sumacs that, in winter and spring, resemble twisting candles with stylized red flames. Turn right and look to your right as you climb. This part of the trail is elevated, allowing you to look through the trees and over a little wooded valley. Turn right at marker U2 onto a narrow trail leading down into that little valley, watching for pricker bushes and poison ivy. You can still hear the muted sounds of cars on the Beltline, but otherwise this part of the Arboretum feels very private.

Continue on the narrow uphill trail, marked by patches of emerald moss, and into another section of pines. If you're walking late in the day, the sun shines through the trees in a satisfyingly dramatic way. There's a feeling of age and history in the ridged bark of a 70-foot-tall white pine. Bear left one last time and follow the piney path up a low rise to the parking lot.

RESOURCES

- *The Arboretum* (University of Wisconsin–Madison Arboretum, 1981), a booklet published more than 20 years ago, doesn't include recent developments, but it's an interesting place to begin reading about Madison's favorite green space.

- www.madnorski.org/arboretum.html
  This website is sponsored by Madison Nordic Ski Club, but its maps and information are useful for walkers as well as cross-country skiers within the Arboretum.

- wiscinfo.doit.wisc.edu/arboretum
  The official website of the Arboretum, with a calendar of
  events, tours, articles, classes, and more. Check out the
  wonderful compilation of field notes written by Arboretum
  naturalists, who tromp through every nook and cranny.
  The notes are evocative, funny, and always extremely
  informative.

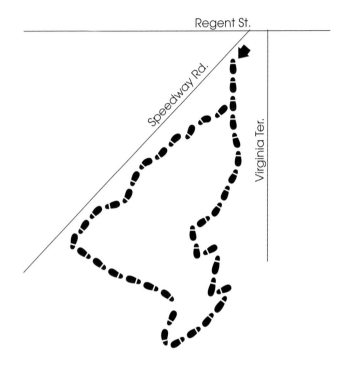

6. Forest Hill Cemetery

People usually consider walking on water or in thin air a miracle. But I think the real miracle is not to walk either on water or in thin air, but to walk on earth.
—Thich Nhat Hanh

1 Speedway Road

Natural interest, historical
            interest
Length: About 1.5 miles;
            30 minutes to
            1 hour
Loop: Yes
Terrain: Hilly, with easy
            paved paths;
            accessible to
            strollers and
            wheelchairs

Children are drawn to cemeteries, at least the children
we've known. Our neighbor's three-year-old son used
to have a charmingly evocative name for the cemetery
in our neighborhood: Sadlands.

We know it as Forest Hill Cemetery. Here lie
generations of Madison's finest politicians, merchants,
intelligentsia, and ordinary folk. Forest Hill is a city
park, and it feels like a park—a well-tended, grassy
park that just happens to be full of gravestones. Our
youngest daughter still begs for walks through the
cemetery's winding, tree-lined paths. She likes to skip
across the lush green fields, stopping at headstones
and making up stories about the lives of the people
buried there.

Maps of Forest Hill Cemetery are available at the
cemetery office, if it's open. And while it's helpful to
have a map, it's just as acceptable to wander, unled,
through the grassy dips and rises.

Start your walk heading uphill past the cemetery office. To your left, in section 34, are the resting places of a number of Union and Confederate soldiers from the Civil War. They're near one another, appropriately, in two sections separated by a mausoleum with beautiful stained-glass windows. You can imagine the blood and sweat and tears of these men who lived long ago, linking them together forever.

The Confederate soldiers were prisoners of war who never made it home. They died at Camp Randall and were buried here. Look for one grave set slightly apart from the rows of identical small white headstones, where Alice Whiting Waterman is buried. Waterman was a widow who came to Madison from Louisiana after the Civil War to manage the Vilas House Hotel. Appalled by the way the Confederate graves were neglected, Waterman tended the graves (on her own nickel) for 30 years, until she died in 1897. Now she's buried in the Confederate Rest with the rest of her "boys."

The cemetery is full of stories, all of them little windows onto the past. Of course you know how each and every one of them ends—but don't we all know that anyway? There's every style of marker here, from flat stones subsiding into the welcoming ground, their letters very nearly worn away, to weathered gray knee-high memorials to towering architectural monuments. There are stones made from granite, stones etched with complicated laser illustrations, plaques in bronze, thick black marble slabs. There are children's graves, short stone pillars topped with a carving of a sleeping lamb.

Walking through rows of weathered stones, you have the sense of slowly scrolling by hundreds of lives. It's a bittersweet feeling, a reminder that life doesn't last forever. It's also a peaceful one. Here in the middle of the hustle and bustle of ever-changing life, the cemetery stays the same. Occasionally you see a fresh grave, an irregular patch of rich brown midwestern dirt, littered with drying bunches of flowers or newly bare to the elements. But you won't see many, since Forest Hill Cemetery is nearly full.

Head uphill past the mausoleum on your left and bear right. Section 21, on your left, holds the graves of many of the families whose names grace street signs, parks, and schools all over Madison. One of these is Simeon Mills (1810–1895), one of Madison's first settlers, who was at various times justice of the peace, state senator, a University of Wisconsin regent, and trustee of the State Hospital for the Insane.

Pass section 23 on the left, and turn left at the near end of section 18. Head toward the back of the cemetery, keeping straight where the road forks. In

section 19, on your right, lies the grave of a Madisonian we should all be thankful for: Stephen Babcock (1843–1931) invented a butterfat test that (according to a pamphlet put out by Historic Madison) revolutionized the dairy industry. You can judge for yourself by tasting Babcock Hall ice cream, the brand made by the university's agricultural school, where Babcock was a professor of agricultural chemistry for many years.

Plenty of famous Madisonians are buried at Forest Hill, including Harry Steenbock, who discovered vitamin D; John Olin, founder of the Madison parks system; Robert "Fighting Bob" La Follette, a congressman, governor, and U.S. senator who ran for president as a Progressive in 1924; and Charles Van Hise, a professor of geology and one-time president of the university.

Turn left at the far end of section 20, and take the next right. Section 14 is on your right. Continue along to the far end of section 35 on your right. The discriminating observer can make out three of the state's 4,000 or so effigy mounds. The mounds—earthworks that form recognizable shapes when seen from above—were constructed by a group of indigenous people known as the mound builders about a thousand years ago. Who were the mound builders, and why did they build mounds shaped like geese, panthers, thunderbirds, foxes, eagles, and other

animals? No one knows, although any number of theories have been floated through the years—burial chambers (a few effigy mounds contain human remains), ceremonial objects, living sculptures.

Unless you know that the grassy hump at the back of section 35 is a mound in the shape of a goose, you wouldn't notice. Once you know, it takes on a poignant, peaceful quality. We may not understand this message from the past, but we feel its power anyway.

In addition to being the site of two panther mounds, section 35 also contains the remains of many local veterans from some of the more recent U.S. wars, beginning with the Spanish-American War of 1898 and including vets from World War I, World War II, the Korean War, and Vietnam.

Follow the road, which curves around section 35, and head back uphill. Notice the contrast between the old graves in section 35 and the newer ones in section 41, on your left. The newer section looks very much like a well-mowed field, festooned here and there with bunches of flowers; the headstones here are nearly flush to the ground, to facilitate mowing and maintenance.

Turn left at section 38 and head straight down the hill. Section 10, on your right, is one of three Jewish sections in the cemetery. At the far edge of section 10, look for the grave of Manfred Swarsensky (1906–1981), a Holocaust survivor who helped found Temple Beth El, Madison's reform synagogue. Swarsensky was the rabbi at Beth El for 36 years, and was well known in and around Madison for his humanitarian and ecumenical works. Most of those 36 years are documented in annual confirmation photos in Beth El's lower level. There you can see Rabbi Swarsensky age, year by year, growing grayer and smaller in every picture.

The best way to find Rabbi Swarsensky's grave is to look for a headstone with many smaller stones on top of it. Some people believe that the custom of leaving a pebble on top of a headstone dates from a time when Jewish people buried their dead in the desert, piling up stones to keep wild animals from getting at the bodies. Wherever it came from, modern Jews consider it a sign of respect to mark their visit to a grave by leaving a stone.

Keep going uphill until you have to turn one way or the other. Turn right, passing section 42 on your left, and continue on to section 39, also on your left. This part of the cemetery, close to Speedway Road, is one of the last open sections. Many of the new graves here belong to Hmong people, hill people from Laos and one of Wisconsin's fastest-growing immigrant groups. Since the end of the Vietnam War, more than 150,000 Hmong people have made their way to America, and a significant number have settled in Wisconsin.

Make sure you walk all the way around the Hmong gravestones, because a few are elaborately decorated on the back with multicolored laser carvings showing images of peaceful mountains and woods, meant to represent the deceased's life in a lost homeland half a world away.

Follow the road, bearing left, past sections 8 and 32 on your left. Continue straight, passing the monolith to the Vilas family on your left in section 31. William Freeman Vilas was a Civil War veteran and U.W. regent who was close friends with President Grover Cleveland; Vilas Park is named after his son Henry. His wife, Anna, was a philanthropist and close friend of President Cleveland's wife. William's father, Levi, moved to Madison from Vermont in 1851 and became mayor of Madison in 1861.

Bear left again, keeping section 30 on your left. On your right, in section 29, look for the grave of Daniel Tenney, marked by a large round sphere set on a square base. Tenney was a prominent lawyer in Chicago who later founded Tenney Park in Madison.

Finish your tour of the cemetery with a stop at the grave of one of America's most famous historians, in section 30. Frederick Jackson Turner was a Pulitzer Prize–winning historian whose theory of the frontier helped define America to itself and the world 100 years ago. He was a professor of history at the University of Wisconsin from 1891 until 1908, when the board of regents complained that he spent too much time doing research and not enough time teaching. (Some things never change, apparently.) According to a booklet about the cemetery called *Forest Hill Cemetery: A Biographical Guide to the Ordinary and the Famous Who Shaped Madison and the World,* Turner, "wishing to spare his friend President Van Hise and himself humiliation…quietly made his unhappiness known and was enthusiastically offered a position by Harvard, which seized the opportunity to make a spectacular improvement in its history program. After a near faculty rebellion, the regents agreed to stay out of basic academic operations in the future."

RESOURCES

- *Forest Hill Cemetery: A Biographical Guide to the Ordinary and the Famous Who Shaped Madison and the World* (Historic Madison, Inc., 1996).
  An 83-page book about the cemetery and its denizens.

- *A Biographical Guide to Forest Hill Cemetery* (Historic Madison, Inc., 2002).
  This revised and expanded two-volume set has everything you want to know about the cemetery and those buried there. A fabulous resource for both the merely curious and the historically inclined.

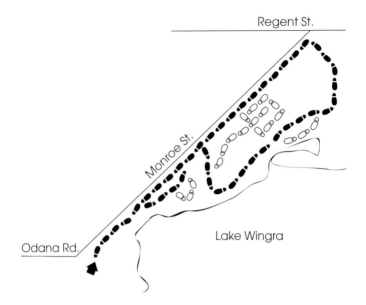

Regent St.

Monroe St.

Odana Rd.

Lake Wingra

7. Monroe Street End to End

Take a two-mile walk every morning before breakfast.
—Harry Truman (advice on how to live to be 80,
on his 80th birthday)

Monroe Street and Odana Road

Family friendly, eating, ice cream
Length: About 3 miles; 1 to 2 hours
Loop: Yes
Terrain: Easy pavement and path; accessible to
wheelchairs and strollers

Monroe Street is the near west side's version of State
Street, with a little more of the natural world thrown
in. Like so much of Madison's urban geography, it
doesn't extend straight north-south or east-west but
tilts, running roughly southwest to northeast. Back in
1838, Monroe Street was Madison's first official public
road; it was called Monroe Road because it led toward
the town of Monroe, about 45 miles away. By the
1890s it had become a street, reflecting the shift from
rural to urban. These days more than 20,000 cars a
day speed down Monroe Street.

Start at the southwest end, where you can park in a
small wooded lot bordering a section of the
Arboretum. Four thousand years ago, this area was
probably a Native American hunting and fishing
camp; now the Arboretum and the neighborhood are
working to restore it to oak savanna.

Head northeast on Monroe past Mallatt's, a drugstore
famous for its extravagant selection of Halloween
costumes. The Plough Inn at 3402 Monroe, part of the
Arbor House Bed and Breakfast, is one of the oldest
buildings still standing in Madison. Built in the 1850s,
it was once a tavern and stagecoach stop on the old
Monroe Road.

Just up the street at 3200, the Gothic-style Dudgeon
Center sits at the top of a steep embankment like a
castle on a hillside. Back in the 1920s, this part of
Madison was expanding rapidly, and the Dudgeon
Center was built as an elementary school. Nowadays
the building houses a nursery school, a private school,
and a handful of community programs, and you can

still step inside and find marvelous details from the past. Look for three tiles showing characters from "Old King Cole" in the original kindergarten room, and for tiles depicting animals over each water fountain (at child's-eye level, of course).

Continue up Monroe for another couple of blocks. Knickerbocker Place, on your right, is a recent addition to the neighborhood, built in the 1990s; as small shopping areas go, it's one of the nicer ones. Milward Farrell Fine Art has a wonderful selection of jewelry, lamps, and other art for sale, but we don't recommend taking children inside—there are too many exquisite but highly breakable objects. Studio You, on the other hand, is a great place to spend a couple of hours with kids. Put on a smock, buy a piece of unglazed pottery, and paint to your heart's content. When you're hungry, Bluephie's is only a hop, skip, and a jump away, serving an extensive menu in a child-friendly atmosphere.

There are a number of good restaurants on this stretch of Monroe Street, including Pasqual's (2534), which serves burritos, tacos, and other southwestern fare. Michael's Frozen Custard is the most frequently requested destination for out-of-town visitors (at least in our household). Order soft-serve cones and sit

under an umbrella, where you can schmooze and watch the world go by. Or take your ice cream around back and through the fence to the playground in Wingra Park. You can also rent canoes and pedal boats at the kiosk by Lake Wingra during the summer.

A few blocks east, Edgewood College, a private Catholic school, dominates the block between Edgewood Avenue and Woodrow Street. Built as a villa for a wealthy Philadelphia lawyer, the original building was home to Wisconsin Governor Cadwallader Washburn and his wife in the 1870s. The Washburns gave it to the Dominican Sisters of Sinsinawa, who started an elementary and high school for girls here in the early 1880s. It's been a school in some way, shape, or form ever since. Take a short detour to wander across the elegant campus, with its rolling lawn, huge trees, and beautiful landscaping.

Back on Monroe Street, walk to the far end of the Edgewood Campus and turn right onto Edgewood Avenue. This neighborhood is known as Vilas, for the park that's on the other side of the hill, and this section is often referred to as the Presidents, because the streets are named for U.S. presidents. Turn left and follow any one of them parallel to Monroe, admiring the large, lovingly restored old houses. Some of

Madison's best-known residents live in this neighborhood, including jazz musician Ben Sidran and writer Lorrie Moore.

Get back onto Monroe at Van Buren Street. You don't want to miss Relish (1923), a deli serving grilled peanut butter and jelly, roast beef with horseradish aïoli, and other sandwiches. Two doors down, the Seed Savers Exchange (1919) has its only retail store in the United States. Seed Savers is a national organization whose mission is propagating heirloom seeds for antique roses, garlic, prairie plants, bulbs, and thousands of other varieties. Stop in to see the gardening supplies, tools, books, seeds, and wonderful children's section, which are enough to inspire flowery fantasies no matter how black your thumb.

The next two blocks of Monroe are packed with coffee bars, restaurants, and unique stores. Leave yourself plenty of time to discover them all. Our favorites include the Grace Chosy Gallery (1825), an art gallery that shows midwestern artists, and the locally owned Wild Child (1813), a store that specializes in bright, colorful clothes for kids from birth through adolescence. Who could resist a tiny pair of tie-dyed rainbow leggings and matching tee?

Find women's clothes in soft, flowing fabrics and flattering designs at Indigo Moon (1809). Orange Tree Imports (1723) is always our first stop when we're shopping for stocking stuffers, kids' birthday parties, kitchenware, cookbooks, jewelry, and other appealing items. Continue down Monroe to Mickie's Dairy Bar (1511), the closest thing Madison has to a real diner.

The 1500 block of Monroe Street dead-ends into Regent Street. From here you have two choices: Retrace your steps down Monroe Street, or take a slightly more natural route back to the car.

To go with the latter option, start back on Monroe and take the first left onto Oakland, proceeding uphill through the Presidents. At the V just past Adams Street, veer right onto Campbell Street. Take Campbell to Mound Park, a large grassy hump at the center of a traffic circle. The Native American mound builders who once lived here marked the site of an effigy mound by tying down a sapling. See if you can find the marker tree here, in the northeast corner of this little park. Better yet, see if you can find the animal mound. (Hint: *Bear* left.)

Take Vilas Avenue to Garfield and turn left. One block takes you to Vilas Park, a veritable paradise for the small set with not one but two great playgrounds. (You can't miss the slide shaped like a giant psychedelic shoe.) Head across the park toward the stone bridge, which leads you to the Vilas Park Zoo, Madison's free city zoo and a day trip unto itself. The children's zoo features goat-feeding and camel rides.

When you're through with the zoo, come back
through the park and turn left onto Edgewood Drive
where it meets Edgewood Avenue, at the foot of a
very steep hill. Edgewood Drive quickly becomes a
two-way road. Local residents have been trying to
have it made into a no-car zone for years, but for
now it's open to vehicles. Lake Wingra, on your left,
is (despite its small size) one of the top five muskie
lakes in the state.

The nice thing about this part of the walk is how
secluded it feels. You're only a block or two away from
houses and busy streets, but you might be walking
through woods on a summer or snowy evening. Pass
the Edgewood Grade School and look for the
Mazzuchelli (that's Matzah-KELLY) Biological Station
on your right. Researchers come to Mazzuchelli from
Edgewood College, the Yahara Watershed Network,
and the University of Wisconsin to study air, water,
and land resources.

Go down the steps leading to Mazzuchelli and follow the wood-chipped path around the center and onto a short pier with a great view of Lake Wingra. From this spot you can imagine the lake as it was more than a thousand years ago, when the mound builders lived here.

Come back to the present and follow the path back up the hill to the road. After a short distance the road bends to the right and becomes Woodrow Street. From the bottom of Woodrow, you're only a hop, skip, and jump away from Vilas Park—but since there's no public footpath through the yards of the houses here (and since the residents here have steadfastly refused to allow one) you have to walk about a quarter mile to get back to Vilas Park.

You don't mind, because you're on a walking tour, after all. Follow Woodrow back up to Monroe and turn left for a short block or two. When you're back on the block with the park, turn left onto the bike path that leads through the playground. Wind your way through Wingra Park and onto Arbor Drive, a quiet street that parallels Monroe, past Temple Beth El, Madison's only Reform synagogue.

Pick up the bike path again just before Arbor Drive ends, bearing left before the parking lot. Turn left at a sign for the Kenneth Jensen Wheeler Council Ring, and follow the grassy path through woods and down a set of stone steps, over a stream and into the center of a council ring, a circular gathering place set off by a low wall of stones. The council ring was built in 1938 by Danish landscape architect and conservationist Jens

Jensen. Jensen designed two other council rings in
Madison, one near Liz Waters Hall on the U.W.
campus and one in the Glenway Children's Park not
far from here. This one is named for his grandson, a
landscape architecture student who died of a brain
aneurysm as he was about to graduate from the
university.

Retrace your steps back to the main trail, which leads
you out onto Monroe Street. Turn left again at the light
across from Parman's service station, onto a short,
secluded trail that winds through trees and woodland
plantings and takes you back to the parking lot.

RESOURCES

- *Exploring the Dudgeon-Monroe Neighborhood* (Dudgeon-
  Monroe Neighborhood Association, 1999).
  This useful little booklet is packed with history,
  neighborhood tours, and photographs. For information
  email the association at dmna@fullfeed.com, or visit its
  website, www.dmna.org.

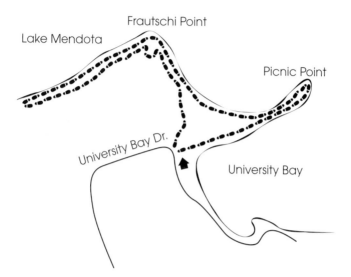

Frautschi Point
Lake Mendota
Picnic Point
University Bay Dr.
University Bay

8. Picnic Point/ Frautschi Point

I only went out for a walk and finally concluded to stay out till sundown, for going out, I found, was really going in.—John Muir

Off University Bay Drive

Natural interest

Length: Picnic Point and back, about 1.2 miles; Picnic Point/Frautschi Point loop, about 3 miles; between 30 minutes and 1 hour

Loop: Yes

Terrain: Mostly flat; wide dirt paths with some narrower trails; not recommended for strollers or wheelchairs

The 0.6-mile walk out to Picnic Point is probably the single best-known walk in town, and for good reason. There's something quintessentially Madisonian about this easy, appealing stroll down a peninsula that pokes into Lake Mendota. It's typical of the closeness between natural places and urban landscape that still exists in this small-to-midsize city. People here take their proximity to green spaces and water and forest seriously, and never for granted.

And they really do picnic at Picnic Point, with children, dogs, and other (sometimes surprising) accoutrements. Take this walk just before sunrise on the first day of May, and you'll find the members of Madison's Morris-dance team cavorting with bells in celebration of May Day.

The walk begins in the parking lot by the water. Pass between two stone pillars that once flanked the gate leading to the home of lumberman Edward J. Young, who bought the area known as Picnic Point Farm in 1925 as a wedding present for his wife, Alice. The house was destroyed by fire in 1935, and Young sold the land to the University of Wisconsin for $205,000.

The well-marked path runs the length of the peninsula. It's mostly dirt, with some gravel and patches of paving, and it can be muddy in spring. But spring is a great time to walk out to Picnic Point. After a long Wisconsin winter, the sounds of birdsong and ice breaking up are true music to the ears.

The path takes you through deciduous woods. To your right, look toward the university, across the sheltered corner of Lake Mendota known as University Bay. Professors and students have been studying the loons, great blue herons, and other fauna and flora here since the turn of the twentieth century. In the last 70 years or so, the forces of development and conservation have butted heads over this marshy area. The compromises they've reached have shaped this part of Lake Mendota's shoreline and created the landscape known as the Campus Natural Area.

About a third of the way up, the peninsula narrows until it's barely wider than the path. Families swim and picnic on the beach to your left, which has an inspiring view of Middleton and Cherokee Marsh. Look for the capitol on your right, rising above the boxy skyline. There are several outdoor fireplaces nearby, where Madison's favorite summer cooking activity—grilling out—can take place, and plenty of benches for those who simply want to sit and admire the view.

Stay on the wide central path, or bear right onto a side path that veers closer to the lake for a slightly woodsier (but still very easy) walk. Friends of the Campus Natural Area, a nonprofit group that helps preserve this part of the university, runs field trips all through here, so don't be surprised if you pass groups of people looking for insects, examining cattails, or otherwise occupied.

The peninsula widens into a knob at the very end. Climb down to the edge of the lake in winter or early spring and see the ice shapes formed by the constantly shifting conjunction of water and shore. In summer or fall, waves lap playfully at the jumbled boulders.

If a short walk is what you're after, head back the way you came to the parking lot, for a total distance of 1.2 miles. If you're up for more, follow the main path back about 0.2 miles, and then bear right onto the wooded side path that leads closer to the water. Continue past two enormous willow trees on your right. Their ridged bark seems ancient, though willows actually grow very quickly (at least measured by tree time). Picnic Point Marsh, on your left, fills up in spring and summer; if the lake rises high enough, this path will be underwater.

Walk along the sandy beach for a while, admiring the driftwood and scrim of stones left behind by the water. This wooded area is fabulous for birding, especially in early spring. Eventually you have to get back onto the Lake Mendota footpath, heading west toward Frautschi Point and Eagle Heights. This path is more "natural" than the Picnic Point path, with many more ups and downs, tree stumps and fallen logs, but is still a fairly easy walk.

As the path turns to the north, you'll pass the Biocore Prairie, five acres of abandoned fields being restored to prairie by students in U.W.'s Biocore 302 class. Bear right toward Frautschi Point. In 1990, John and Jerry Frautschi donated the land to the University of Wisconsin, and the name was changed, but some people still call it by its original name, Second Point. Keep bearing right, toward the water. There's no sign to tell you when you've reached the main point, but there is an old stone fireplace and a wide, panoramic view of Lake Mendota, including the capitol.

From Frautschi Point, you have a choice: For a longer walk, continue along the lakeside path for another three-quarters of a mile or so, until you come out in Eagle Heights, a section of university housing. From there you can walk back along the road to the Picnic Point parking lot.

If you're ready to head for home, take a slightly different route. Bear left along a path that was paved long ago; you'll see and feel traces of asphalt underfoot. Turn left onto a side path that leads to a spectacular oak. This huge crowned tree is a vision of arboreal majesty. Veer 90 degrees left at the oak and follow a little wooded path. Turn right onto the path you came in on, and then, about 80 feet later, bear right at a sign reading "Lake Mendota Frautschi Point Alternate Trail to Picnic Point."

Follow this trail through woods and up a rise until you're back at the Biocore Prairie. Turn right, away from the lake, and head uphill. On your left is an outdoor kiln owned and sporadically fired up by university students. At the paved road, turn right. This area of tall hemlock and white pines is a natural spot for birding. Follow the road, bearing left downhill, until you arrive back at the Picnic Point parking lot.

RESOURCES

- www.uwalumni.com/fcna
  Website run by Friends of the Campus Natural Area. Site includes history, photographs, information on "field trips," related links, and more. An excellent resource for anyone interested in this part of Madison's lakeshore.

- www.uwalumni.com/fcna/newsletter/10_01/newsletter3.htm
  Website with information on the Biocore Prairie Restoration.

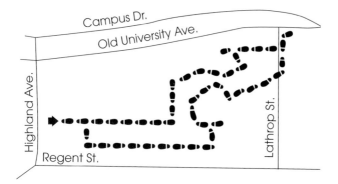

9. University Heights

Thoughts come clearly while one walks.
—Thomas Mann

Van Hise Avenue and Highland Avenue

Historical interest, family friendly
Length: About 1.5 miles; 30 minutes to 1 hour
Loop: Yes
Terrain: Pavement and city streets; accessible to
         wheelchairs and strollers; very steep in spots

Put on your sneakers, stretch your calves, and get
ready to take a walk on the steep side. University
Heights is one of Madison's hilliest and most historic
neighborhoods. Back in the 1890s, it was a distant
suburb of downtown Madison, and it took a certain
amount of *je ne sais quoi* to set down metaphorical tent
stakes so far from civilization. Now University Heights
is considered practically downtown, and all it takes to

own a home here is a couple hundred thousand dollars.

Begin your walking tour on the fringe of the Heights, in the part of town known as the Regent neighborhood, for its proximity to Regent Street. Park on a side street and find your way to the corner of Van Hise and Highland, directly across from West High School. Walk east on Van Hise, admiring the profusion of gardens along these blocks. Some are "wild" gardens, and some feature more traditional plantings, but all are scrupulously well maintained and wonderful to look at. Along with the gardens, you'll see a variety of architectural styles, from pseudo-farmhouses to classy brick boxes to stately Victorians with wraparound porches.

Cross Ash Street and look for 2222 Van Hise, a gray Craftsman-style house where naturalist and conservationist Aldo Leopold spent the last 24 years of his life. According to the plaque out front, Leopold

was "probably the most quoted voice in the history of conservation." Some might see irony in the fact that this once-modest home now boasts a Jacuzzi and was on the market recently for half a million dollars. What would Leopold have thought of that?

Continue east on Van Hise across Allen Street, the western boundary of University Heights. You'll know you've crossed over because the houses east of Allen are larger, and most sit on bigger plots. At the corner of Bascom and Van Hise, don't miss the Storybook House (2114 Van Hise), a whimsical "cottage" (actually a substantial house) set back from the street on a wooded plot rife with Solomon's seal, astilbe, jewelweed, and other plants you'd expect to find in the woods, not in someone's front yard. Its cream-colored walls and playful candy-striped teal shutters really do make it look like a house from a fairy tale.

Right next door as you continue up Van Hise is one of the most spectacular historic houses in Madison. The Bradley House, at 106 N. Prospect Avenue, was built

in 1910 by architect Louis H. Sullivan, who designed
and built skyscrapers and large-scale buildings in
Chicago and other cities. This striking Prairie-style
building was one of Sullivan's few residential designs.
Its flowing base, unusual features, and mix of brick,
shingles, and wood give it an imposing air. Built for
the daughter of a plumbing magnate and her husband,
Dr. Harold C. Bradley, the house was sold in 1914 to
Sigma Phi fraternity. This unlikeliest of frat houses
became a National Historic Landmark in 1976.

Turn left onto North Prospect and admire the front
view of Bradley House. North Prospect curves around
to the right, confusingly; take the left fork, which is
Forest Street. The black iron railing on your right
marks the edge of the property that is home to
whoever is the current chancellor of the university
(but more on that later).

Head downhill and turn right onto Chamberlain,
where you immediately head uphill again, along
another edge of the chancellor's property. Many of the
houses in this neighborhood were and still are home
to professors at the university. The Ross House (2021
Chamberlain), for instance, was once the abode of
Professor Edward A. Ross, who headed U.W.'s
department of sociology from 1906 to 1937. Ross was
an outspoken critic of the abuses of big business, the
gold standards, and the exploitation of Chinese
railroad workers.

Follow Chamberlain until it branches to the left; stay
to the right, which is Arlington Place. This block-long
street boasts four houses designed by Claude and

Starck, one of Madison's top architectural firms at the turn of the twentieth century. The Whitson House at 1920 Arlington, a beautiful stucco, was built for soils professor Andrew Whitson in 1905. Down the block at 1902, the Jennings House—a spectacular and very large Chicago Progressive–style house—combines historical design features with then-modern elements. It was built in 1903 by John T.W. Jennings, who was the supervising architect for the university as well as for his own house.

Across the street at the corner of Arlington and North Prospect is the Turneaure House (166 N. Prospect), designed in 1905 so that every main room in the house has a fabulous view of the campus and Lake Mendota. Turn left onto North Prospect again and go downhill. Take a short break in front of the immense Tudor-style Pence House (168 N. Prospect), home to

several university professors between 1909 and the
present. Then follow North Prospect another block,
stopping at the corner of Spooner to admire the Ely
House (205 N. Prospect). Richard T. Ely was a well-
known professor at U.W., once hailed by the *New York
Times* as "the dean of American economics."
This early Georgian revival house was designed for
Ely and his wife in 1896 by Chicago architect Charles
Sumner Frost.

Across the street at 220 N. Prospect is the Moores
House, a later Georgian revival built in 1923 by local
architect Frank Riley. Riley designed a number of
houses in and around Madison; this one was
commissioned by local lawyer John M. Olin for his
nephew, Howard Moores.

Turn right onto Kendall Avenue, crossing to the south
side of the street to see three equally impressive
architectural examples. Knowlton House (1717
Kendall) is one of the oldest houses in the Heights, a
gorgeous Queen Anne with turquoise trim and a big
porch. It was built in 1895, when Kendall Avenue was
still a dirt road bordering a cornfield, and it housed
English professor Amos Knowlton, his wife, and their
five children in semirural splendor.

Next door at 1711 Kendall is Smith House, an early
Georgian revival built in 1896. While the house is
quite spectacular, it's the details that wow you—ornate
swags over the windows, a row of calla lilies planted
along the front walk.

Art Rules

A brief detour brings you to one of Madison's best-kept secrets—the gallery at the Wisconsin Academy of Sciences, Arts and Letters (1922 University). The Academy was founded in 1870 to "connect people and ideas from all walks of life to celebrate thought and culture" around Wisconsin. Pretty heady stuff, but then this *is* Wisconsin.

This small but elegant gallery shows top-notch work by Wisconsin painters, photographers, and artists. (And it's air-conditioned, which makes it a welcome oasis on a hot summer's day.) To get there, head north on North Prospect until it ends at University Avenue. Cross University and turn left until you come to 1922.

The last house on the block is Kahlenberg House (234 Lathrop), built a few years later than the other two but every bit as imposing. This Queen Anne–style house features Gothic elements—paired porch columns, pointed arch windows on the third floor—and was home to Professor Louis Kahlenberg, a pioneer in the field of physical chemistry.

Turn left onto Lathrop and walk a short block to the
First Congregational Church (1609 University), a
Georgian revival built in the late 1920s and modeled
after churches built in London by seventeenth-century
architect Christopher Wren.

Head back up Lathrop (and we do mean up), past
Kendall, and turn right onto Summit. Halfway up the
block on your right is Sloan House (1712 Summit), a
Tudor revival dating from 1927 and still one of the
largest houses in the neighborhood. Sinclair Lewis
lived here in 1940, during a brief teaching stint at the
university.

Cross Spooner Street and get ready for a real climb.
The 1800 block of Summit may just be the steepest
residential block in Madison. Turn right at the next
street, Ely Place, and stop to admire the very modern-
looking Morehouse House (101 Ely), built in 1937. Its
boxy shape, flat roofs, and abstract design make it a
perfect example of the international style of
architecture.

Two doors down at 115 Ely is Buell House, our
favorite house in the Heights, the one we fantasize
about living in if, say, we won the lottery. The first
house built in this part of the Heights in 1894, it
stood alone for years, and was known as Buell's Folly
after its owners, Charles and Martha Buell.
Constructed by the same architects who built the Red
Gym on Langdon Street, Buell House is the very
picture of late Victorian magnificence, with its deep
red shingles and rich detailing.

Tear your eyes away and step across the street to
Gilmore House (120 Ely), also known as the Airplane
House. Built in 1908 by the great Frank Lloyd Wright
himself, this house features two copper-roofed side
"wings" on either side of a triangular balcony that
looks like the nose of a jet—hence the nickname.

Ely Place feeds into North Prospect. Next door to the
Airplane House is the Elliott House (137 N. Prospect).
This Prairie-style home dates from 1910, and makes a
nice visual break from the late Victorians and 1930s
houses here.

If you keep going down North Prospect, you'll pass
the front of the brick house that houses the chancellor
of the university. Known as Olin House, this brick
English-style mansion is one of the least visually
interesting houses in the Heights, despite its imposing
yard. So instead, turn left onto Roby and follow it
downhill to another confusing intersection. Keep

curving to the left,
across Van Hise,
and walk east for
a glimpse of one
of the most
unusual (and
modern) houses
in the Heights at
1833 Van Hise.
Built by the
owners of the
Soap Opera on
State Street, this
relatively recent

addition to the neighborhood takes full advantage of its oddly shaped lot.

Head back to Roby and follow its curve south to Chadbourne. You're at Olive Jones Park, which is also part of the playground for Randall Elementary School. The redbrick Tudor revival–style school building was constructed in 1906, and currently serves about 400 third-, fourth-, and fifth-graders.

Turn right onto Chadbourne and head west. These houses look positively minimalist after the mansions on the hill. Stay on Chadbourne until it dead-ends at West High School. Directly in front of you on the school grounds is "Path of Voices," a multimedia sculpture by Brad McCallum. "Path of Voices" is one of five installations at high schools around Madison designed to make people more aware of the roots of violence. Five granite slabs stand upright in a loose ring; built-in speakers continuously play oral histories and testimonials (many of which are disturbing) recorded by local high school students.

Turn right onto Ash and left onto Van Hise to get back to the beginning of the walk.

RESOURCES

- *The University Heights Historic District: A Walking Tour* (Madison Landmarks Commission and the Regent Neighborhood Association, 1987).
  If you want to know even more about the history of the Heights, this pamphlet has it all, including photographs, a map, and a self-guided walking tour.

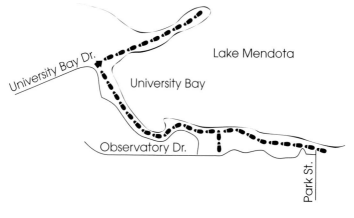

Lake Mendota

University Bay Dr.

University Bay

Observatory Dr.

Park St.

10. Lakeshore Path Walk

*There is nothing like walking to get the feel of a country.
A fine landscape is like a piece of music; it must be taken
at the right tempo. Even a bicycle goes too fast.*
—Paul Scott Mowrer

Off University Bay Drive

Natural interest, family friendly
Length: 3.2 miles; 1 to 1-1/2 hours
Loop: No
Terrain: Flat, wide dirt paths with a few narrower side
         trails; accessible to strollers and wheelchairs

Combine this walk with a jaunt out to the end of
Picnic Point, or make it a separate destination on a

lazy Sunday afternoon. Start at the Picnic Point parking lot and head east along the lake on the Howard M. Temin Lakeshore Path, named for the U.W. oncologist who shared the 1975 Nobel Prize in medicine. Temin walked or biked the path every day, summer and winter; some locals believe the lakeshore path was one of the enticements that kept him in Madison. Dr. Temin died in 1994, and four years later the path was dedicated in his name.

Whatever it's called, the path follows the loops and wriggles of the lakeshore, offering teasing glimpses of Lake Mendota, an up-close view of an effigy mound, and sweepingly beautiful broad vistas. Benches at a few of these viewpoints give you the chance to rest— but make sure you've got plenty of mosquito repellent in summer. There's a reason why people refer to the mosquito as the Wisconsin state bird.

In spring and summer, fishing boats large and small trawl the open water and the marshier inland bays. Keep an eye out for a V-shaped wave moving across the water—that's the telltale sign of a muskrat swimming from den to shore. On rare winter days when the conditions are just right (little snow, very cold temperatures, not much wind), watch for iceboats whipping across on the frozen surface of the lake like toy boats zoomed by a large, invisible hand.

The path is paved at first, but asphalt soon gives way to packed dirt. Used by hundreds of university folks each day, the path is well traveled and maintained. The commuter traffic (on foot and on two wheels) makes this a great walk for people-watching, too. If you're lucky, you'll spot well-muscled university students (male and female) training on stationary rowing machines. Little side trails leave the main path, but they all connect back to the main path quickly, so you really can't get lost.

One detour well worth your time can be found by turning right just before the crew building. Head one block south to the corner of Babcock and Observatory Drive, and turn in at the gate to the Allen Centennial Gardens, named for U.W. botanist Ethel Allen and her husband, bacteriologist Oscar Allen. The lavish Victorian house rising from the surrounding gardens is known by various names, including the Lake Dormer, the Fred House (for former university president Edwin B. Fred), and 10 Babcock Drive. Once home to the first four deans of the College of Agricultural and Life Sciences, it now houses the offices of the Agricultural Research Stations.

The gardens, which serve as an outdoor classroom for the horticulture department, are free and open to the public. Depending on the time of year, you'll see all manner of fantastic flowering and nonblooming plants here, from golden daylilies and spikes of deep blue

delphiniums to thick, formal boxwood parterres cut
into fleur-de-lis.

Head back to the lakeshore path and follow it around
the Limnology Lab building (bikers bear right, walkers
left) and up the hill. You've made it to one of
Madison's ultimate destinations—the Wisconsin
Union, which has been called the heart and soul of
the university. Generations of students have hung out
on the Memorial Union Terrace, watching sailboats
and windsurfers glide across Lake Mendota, listening
to live bands, and (of course) drinking beer and eating
brats. You can amuse yourself (and your children)
here for quite a while, feeding the many ducks that
call this sheltered shoreline home. Inside the Union,
make a beeline for the ice cream shop, where you can
get a cone piled with scoops of Babcock Hall ice
cream, made by and named for the agriculture school.
Take your ice cream to a chair on the terrace, where
you can people-watch, listen in on fascinating
conversations, and just relax.

RESOURCES

- www.hort.wisc.edu/garden2001/default.htm
  This website tells you everything you want to know about
  the Allen Centennial Gardens, from what's blooming when
  to how to reserve the garden for a special event.

- www.hoofers.org
  Home page for the Wisconsin Hoofers, which hosts sailing,
  riding, scuba, mountaineering, and other outdoor activities
  for adults and children.

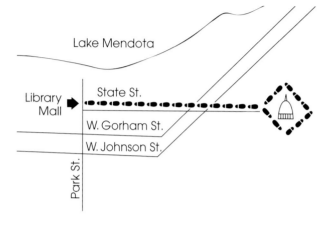

11. State Street

The best remedy for a short temper is a long walk.
—Jacqueline Schiff

Library Mall

Family friendly, restaurants, shopping
Length: About 2 miles; 30 minutes to 1-1/2 hours
Loop: No
Terrain: Flat, easy city streets; accessible to strollers
         and wheelchairs

In the age of big box stores and super malls, cities
large and small struggle to sustain a dynamic, vibrant
downtown. So far, Madison has been one of the lucky
few that's managed to hang on. Its quintessentially
urban identity can be summed up in two words:
State Street.

State Street comprises about 10 blocks, beginning on
campus not far from Memorial Union and ending at

the gloriously domed capitol. In those 10 blocks are innumerable restaurants, coffee bars, and specialty shops. You name it, and you can probably buy it somewhere on State Street.

Start at the Library Mall fountain, which has the words "Teachers and books are the springs from which flow the waters of knowledge" carved inside its stone perimeter. It's an appropriate legend for a downtown walk that includes at least three bookstores.

The first is Paul's Books (670 State), one of our favorite places to hunt up used books on just about any subject, from anatomy to European history to postwar poetry. The Sunroom Café (638), down the street and upstairs, is one of three restaurants in town that once had the word *sun* in their names. Alas, now there are only two. Order an herbal tea, sit at the window, and stare down as town and gown skateboard, stroll, bike, and loiter.

Tomboy Girl (551) caters to fans of local singer/songwriter Tret Fure. This little store (and growing brand) helps support Fure's eponymous record label.

Across the street, Peacock (512) sells lovely little things: beaded purses, boxes, jeweled lamps, and clothes for women. The Exclusive Company (508) has arguably the best collection of music in Madison, with

CDs, DVDs, and even vinyl featuring everything from Limp Biskit to Kiri Te Kanawa. So what if the basement smells a little musty? It's all part of the experience.

Madison had very few Japanese restaurants when we moved here in the early 1990s. Now it has half a dozen, and many people think Wasabi (449) is the best of the bunch. The sushi is definitely worth the walk upstairs.

There are days when you need a hat. Not just any hat, but a hat that seems like it was made for your head. So stop in at Sacred Feather (417). This little store carries every kind of hat you can imagine and some you can't, from baseball caps to collapsible silk top hats. Started as a pushcart in 1975 by a couple of bearded hippie types, the store now combines the flavor of tie-dye with upscale chic.

Next door you'll find the Not Quite Perfect Store (411), full of catalogue overstocks, seconds, and other cheaper-than-usual goodies from Lands' End in nearby Dodgeville. And next door to that, shop for martini glasses, photo frames, kitchenware, throw rugs, and tchotchkes galore at Tellus Mater (409). (Yes, you really do need that pair of *Wind in the Willows* bookends.)

By now you're probably thirsty, so stop for a smoothie at Jamba Juice (401). You can't miss its sunny orange walls. Then cross the street to the Community Pharmacy (341), a cooperatively owned pharmacy that specializes in natural and alternative products. Like so many of the city's cultural landmarks, the Community Pharmacy started in the 1970s and survives in part because of Madison's thriving ex-hippie population. While you're browsing the red clover and black cohosh, the children among you can step next door to Chocolate Coyote, which serves all the usual flavors of ice cream plus exotic offerings like green tea.

Up the block, the legacy of the sixties continues at Ragstock (329), a clothing store beloved by twenty-first-century teens. Tie-dye, vintage-style, midriffs, hip-huggers—yup, they're all here. Across the street, Jazzman (340) sells buttery leathers and other upscale clothes for men.

The Soap Opera (319) is one of Madison's most popular shopping destinations. It reminds us of an old-fashioned candy shop. Wander the aisles and admire a rainbow of soaps, Kama Sutra oils, loofahs, Crabtree & Evelyn products, and yellow rubber ducks in every size from teeny to bigger than your head. We always head straight for the display of primal element soap, long blocks of glycerin soap with brightly colored shapes and images embedded within. Buy it by the slice and dress up your bathroom on the cheap.

If you're looking for beautiful and unusual blank cards to send to friends, you can't beat Shakti (320). The store also sells jewelry, incense, pillows, T-shirts, and books on yoga, tarot, healing, Buddhism, New Age, and other spiritually inclined subjects.

You're getting close to the capitol, but you still have two blocks to go. Stop at Noodles & Co. (232), a chain that sells reasonably priced plates of Italian, Thai, Japanese, Chinese, and continental-style pasta. Then step next door to Puzzlebox (230), a toy store specializing in puzzles, stuffed animals, craft kits, and little toys for kids of all ages. Next door in the same building, the Fanny Garver Gallery hosts shows by local and out-of-town artists.

One of our favorite places to buy gifts (for ourselves and others) is Little Luxuries (214), a jewel of a shop selling everything from sushi dishes to bathrobe-and-slipper sets. It definitely caters to women, with velvety scarves, jewelry, beaded barrettes, lotions, elegant hats, and other necessities of the good life. At Bookworks (109), breathe deeply of the irresistible smell of thousands of used hardcovers and paperbacks, on wooden shelves labeled with handwritten white labels. There's a good children's section at the back of the store.

You can't shop State Street without a stop at the House of Wisconsin Cheese (107), a clearinghouse for cheesehead paraphernalia. Your friends will know you've been to Wisconsin when you come home with cheese shaped like a Holstein, Bucky Badger, or a big red W. Less perishable souvenirs include cheesehead hats in various sizes and a model of the state capitol.

Pop into the real capitol for a look at the inside of the only granite dome in the United States (and the only state capitol built on an isthmus). Inside the first-floor rotunda, ooh and ahh at four exquisite mosaic panels created by late nineteenth-century artist Kenyon Cox. Each mosaic is made up of 100,000 glittering pieces of glass. Look up to see "Resources of Wisconsin," a ceiling mural painted inside the 162-foot dome by Edwin Howland Blashfield, an American painter whose career spanned the mid-nineteenth century to the Depression. Ask inside for a free tour of the capitol, offered weekdays and Saturdays at various times during the day.

This walk is not a loop, so you have to turn around and go back the way you came to Library Mall. Lucky you—you get to stroll State Street twice in one day.

The Farmers' Market

The Dane County Farmers' Market is the place to be on Saturday mornings from April to October. It's not just about shopping; it's an experience. What kind of experience depends on how early you arrive. From 6 in the morning to 2 in the afternoon, the four streets that make up Capitol Square are thronged with farmers (organic and otherwise) selling fruit, vegetables, preserves, flowers, meats, and other goodies. Serious shoppers hit the market before 7:30, because by 8:30 the square is a sea of people. Shuffling, sipping, strolling, gossiping people, many pushing strollers and pulling wagons that nip at the heels of the unwary. Fortunately, most folks tend to be in pretty mellow moods, and just go with the flow.

You can buy almost anything here, from farmers who have been selling at the market for close to 30 years and farmers who are brand-new to the business. There are stands belonging to Hmong families and

Amish farmers. There are small organic farmers and bigger commercial farmers. There's a stand selling nothing but goodies made with chili peppers. Just off the Square, where vendors spill over into the cross streets, you can buy an authentic-looking medieval blouse and skirt, have your palms and feet painted with intricate henna designs, and breathe in the scent of lavender ylang-ylang soap.

Our personal farmers' market favorite is the Summer Kitchen, which has had a presence here since 1968. Row after row of luscious jams, jellies, and preserves sparkle in the morning sun, with names that roll off your tongue: Tayberry. Primrose. Marietta. I don't know what a tayberry is, and I don't much care—just the sight of the sweet red jam glistening in its faceted jar makes me happy for the rest of the day.

The specific stands are always changing, offering a cornucopia of goodies. Here's a partial list of what you can buy on Saturday morning:

> Pesto (seven varieties)
> Honey in glass jars. Honey in little plastic squeeze bears. Honey in little ceramic pots.
> Hanging baskets of fuchsia and other flowers
> Goat cheese (with a label that lists, among other ingredients, "love")
> Smoked trout
> Cinnamon rolls
> Heaps of pink radishes, green scallions, spinach, and other vegetables

Orchids in every shade of lavender, violet,
    fuchsia, and white
Mint honey. Clover honey. Wildflower honey.
    Cranberry blossom honey.
Cheese curds (yes, you're in Wisconsin now)
Eight kinds of tomato seedlings
Honey sticks. Beeswax candles.
Baklava
Organic goat feta
Morels (and don't miss the giant carved morel
    rising from the center of the display table like
    a—well, like a giant morel)
Emu products (including meat, feathers, and
    gorgeous dark green eggs)
Cacti
Fresh garlic spaghettini
Farm-raised venison, rabbit, and duck
Bedding plants
Farm-raised bison, which claims to be lower in
    fat, calories, and cholesterol than chicken
Ostrich jerky
Sheep's-milk cheese
Cut flowers
Rosemary kamut rolls

Stepping Off State

A number of downtown streets cross State between Lake Street and the capitol, and they, too, are worth exploring. Here are a few of the fun, funky destinations you'll find just off State.

A Room of One's Own Feminist Bookstore and Coffeehouse, 307 W. Johnson
> The best bumper stickers and T-shirts in town, if you're a left-leaning feminist, plus an excellent selection of books for and by women.

Avol's Bookstore, 240 W. Gilman
> A paradise of used and new books on every topic.

Canterbury Booksellers, 315 W. Gorham
> The grande dame of Madison's independent bookstores is an excellent place to find a book, hear an author, and drink a latte. Upstairs, the Canterbury Inn is a charming bed-book-and-breakfast with six rooms, each with a mural showing scenes from the Chaucer's *Canterbury Tales.*

Mimosa Bookstore, 260 W. Gilman
> Self-help, spirituality, New Age music, healing, Wiccan, pagan resources.

RESOURCES

- www.sacredfeather.com
  Website for Sacred Feather. Don't miss the page devoted to red hats.

- www.wisconsin.gov/state/capfacts/cap_3d_s.html
  A tour of the capitol in photographs.

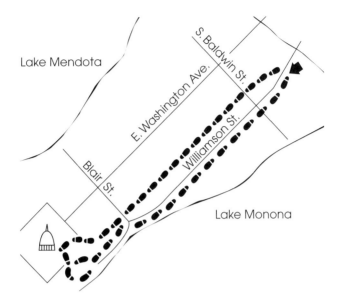

Lake Mendota

S. Baldwin St.

E. Washington Ave.

Williamson St.

Blair St.

Lake Monona

12. Monona Terrace Walk

It is good to collect things; it is better to take walks.
—Anatole France

Williamson Street and the Yahara River

Family friendly, historical interest
Length: About 3 miles; 1 to 2 hours
Loop: Yes
Terrain: Flat, easy pavement; accessible to strollers
and wheelchairs

This quintessentially urban loop swings you through
Madison's near east side, a neighborhood with its own
personal mix of eclectic, artistic, funkadelic styles.

Park on one of the side streets near the Yahara River and Williamson Street—try Thornton or Rogers—and head west on Williamson Street (that's Willy Street to you). Willy Street runs down the isthmus like an artery, continually pumping fresh blood into the city via new restaurants, interesting little shops, and a wonderfully diverse and ever-changing cast of characters.

On the south side of the street, stop by Gayfeather Fabrics, a small but mighty fabric shop owned by Virginia Lienhard. She stocks fabrics like other people stock candy, with a sensuous attention to color and texture. Tear yourself away and continue west on Willy. The near east side is a mix of old Victorians and newer houses, in every state from active disrepair to recently renovated. They're smaller, closer together, and much more colorful than their west side counterparts. Don't miss the deep purple house at 1435-37 Willy; it's right next door to a house with purple and pink trim and across the street from a house with startling hot pink trim. Another purple house, this one a much paler shade with darker trim, can be found at 1415. (See the box on page 119 for more about Madison's purple houses.)

On the next block, wander into RP's Pasta (1353), a little cave of a store that reminds us of a ravioli shop we used to frequent on New York City's Lower East Side. RP's fresh pasta and sauce is every bit as good. Across the street at 1358 is Lazy Jane's Café, one of Madison's top three breakfast restaurants (in our humble opinion). Jane makes thick, buttery scones studded with blackberries, blueberries, and other fruit

that are so good, she limits customers to six scones to go—otherwise she'd run out by 9 a.m.

If you're feeling percussive, stop by Wooden Voices (1438), where you can buy handmade drums in a multitude of sizes, shapes, and styles. Shop for everything else across the street at St. Vincent's Thrift Store, a gold mine of previously owned clothes, toys, books, and household items.

Taking up most of the 1200 block is the venerable Willy Street Co-op, a cooperative grocery store that's been around since the 1970s. You won't see sawdust on the floor or barrels of unchewable grains here, but you will find the best produce in town (much of it organic), fresh seafood, and a truly excellent spot for people-watching.

If you're determined not to indulge yourself, walk right by Lao Laan-Xang (1146), a Laotian restaurant that serves deliciously spicy noodles, curry, and rice dishes. And by all means don't stop at Mother Fool's

Coffeehouse (1101) for a red-eye, Italian soda, or mocha latte.

Take a load off in the Willy Street Park, a tiny urban greenspace at the corner of Brearly and Willy. Then wander across Brearly and into Star Books. Star Books may be one of the smallest indies in town, but it's also one of the nicest.

What could be more urban than a fence? Admire a variety of fence styles and sizes as you stroll by Struck & Irwin Fences (826 Williamson). This two- or three-block section of Willy Street isn't the prettiest part of town, but for those suffering withdrawal pangs from New York, Chicago, or other big cities, it delivers a satisfying shot of gritty urban culture.

Across the street at 805 is Bon Appetit, a cozy little lunch joint with a Mediterranean feel. You could have a bite there, or take it down the block to the old Madison Candy Company building at 744. There the Ground Zero Café, a classic near east side coffeehouse, serves wraps and sandwiches for under $5. The ambience of Ground Zero is a combination of early schoolroom and coffee farm. An old black globe and several vintage clock radios in shades of teal and salmon perch on a windowsill. Pull-down world maps and burlap coffee bags from Costa Rica, the Serengeti, and other locales are pinned up on the walls. A cushy sectional couch tucks into the back corner, lending an air of cozy intellectualism.

Continue west on Willy Street another block. Take a brief but pleasant detour by turning left onto Blount,

crossing Willy, and heading downhill. A short block ends at a little pier directly on Lake Monona. Sit on a bench and watch the water flow into the lake from under the pier, where the Madison Gas and Electric power plant has an outlet. On February days it seems as if every duck in Madison is paddling around in the small semicircle of open water. This is a good spot for a picnic lunch.

Head back up to Willy Street, where you can either turn left onto a wide sidewalk that quickly becomes a bike path or take another short detour to the Gateway Mall, across Willy. This funky little shopping center has three (count 'em) restaurants serving Asian cuisine (Indonesian, Thai, and Chinese). It also has A Woman's Touch, a store you probably don't want to take your children into (even if they *are* in college). Owners Ellen Barnard and Myrtle Wilhite stock a wide variety of erotic accoutrements, all geared toward women's enjoyment.

Get back onto the bike path, which curves to the left at Blair Street, just past Machinery Row. At the turn of the last century, this block-long group of brick buildings held shops full of farm tools. This bike path is one of the most heavily used in town, so keep your eyes open for speeding bikers, bladers, and joggers.

The path curves toward the lake and runs parallel to busy John Nolen Drive. To your left, out in the water,

a white ski jump marks the spot where the Mad-City Ski Team performs for the public free of charge all summer long. When we went to press, shows were scheduled for Sundays at 6 p.m., but check the team's website for details. In winter you can walk out onto the lake and see Kites on Ice, an annual kite festival held on the frozen waters of Lake Monona.

Directly in front of you is a round white building that may remind you of a) a gigantic white wedding cake made out of concrete, or b) the Guggenheim Museum in New York City. Five points if your answer was b), because this is the famous (or infamous) Monona Terrace Community and Convention Center, designed by architect Frank Lloyd Wright, who also created the Guggenheim. Wright's original 1938 design included a rail depot, marina, courthouse, and city hall, and was described in local newspapers as a "dream civic center"; the county board defeated his proposal by a single vote. Fifty-four years and a whole lotta wrangling later, this modified but still impressive confection—I mean convention—center opened its doors.

Turn in at the entrance to a small street-level parking lot and head for the tall blue glass tower. Take the elevator to the very top and get out at the roof garden level. Walk straight through several sets of doors and follow a tiled path outside. The path winds back and forth and eventually brings you to the open-air roof,

which features a fountain, chairs and tables, public bathrooms, and a spectacular view of Lake Monona. On a summer afternoon, the rooftop is populated with businesspeople, young dads with babies, students, wandering conventioneers, and office workers in chairs, their faces lifted in worship to the sun. One out-of-towner, taking in the view below, was overheard to remark, "That's gotta look sharp at night." Indeed it does.

Walk to the southwest end of the rooftop and look back over the path you traveled to get here. The parking lot ramp has the characteristic look of the Guggenheim, white concrete swirls around a central pillar. Head down a level and inside the convention center, where the stairs or elevator will take you down to the main lobby.

The inside of Monona Terrace is largely made up of meeting rooms and banquet halls, but there are a couple of interesting things to see. The Hall of Ideas—

really just a long carpeted hallway—has a permanent
show of photographs of Taliesin West and other
buildings designed by Frank Lloyd Wright. A
fascinating series of black-and-white images shows the
architect himself, late in his life, explaining the
principles of organic architecture through a series of
hand movements, captured on film. We can't say we
understand architecture any better from looking at
those pictures, but they make a good character study.

The gift shop is worth a wander, too, as it's filled with
Wright-inspired tchotchkes, paraphernalia, books, and
other goodies. Tours of Monona Terrace start here
each day at 1 p.m.; there is a small fee.

When you're done admiring Wright's handiwork, go
back to the rooftop level and follow the pedestrian
walkway that leads away from the center and toward
the capitol, connecting up to Martin Luther King
Boulevard. On Wednesday mornings from April to
October there's a farmers' market here, smaller than
the Saturday morning around-the-square version but
still worth a visit. Cross Doty Street, heading for the
capitol, and turn right at the corner of Main Street.
(Look up to see an interesting stonework frieze on one
of the corner buildings.)

Go one short block and take a 45-degree right turn
onto King Street, heading away from the capitol. This
section of town housed Madison's earliest business
district as well as the homes of the pioneers who
created it, and is known as the First Settlement
Neighborhood.

Pick up a free newspaper at 101 King, home of
Isthmus, Madison's weekly alternative newspaper. This
block is a veritable cornucopia of restaurants, all of
them excellent, from Luigi's on the corner to Dog Eat
Dog (yes, it's a hot dog restaurant) to Café
Continental. On the site of the old Madison Hotel,
stop in to Savoir Faire, a good place to browse for
gifts. Two doors down is the historic Majestic Theater,
nearly a century old. Once a movie theater, the
building now houses Club Majestic, a nightclub
featuring dance music, a DJ, and live music.

Continue downhill on King, crossing East Doty, where
you can stop for a quick one at the Great Dane Pub
and Brewing Company. Cross King Street to see the
historical marker on the site of Madison's first
residence, the Peck Cabin. There in 1837, one
Ebenezer Peck and his wife, Rosaline, kept a
boardinghouse, held dancing lessons, and had turtle
soup suppers with the turtles caught out on Mud
Lake—now Lake Mendota. Like all pioneers, the
Pecks faced unexpected hardships, as described in this
diary entry of Rosaline's:

> *The turtles were frozen solid, and rattled together like
> stones, and were put in the cellar to thaw out before we
> could dress them, and, going down a few days after I
> found they had thawed out and were crawling around
> on the bottom of the cellar.*

Alas, the site of this fascinating adventure is now an
office building

Keep going downhill, making a 45-degree left turn onto East Wilson, past the Patchwork Peddler (402 E. Wilson), where you can buy or commission a quilt, and the Cardinal Bar (418), a popular live-music venue with jazz every Sunday night. Follow the sidewalk and the railroad tracks across South Blair, behind Wah Kee, to the east side bike path.

The path runs parallel to and behind Williamson Street, passing the Madison Gas and Electric power plants. As you come up to Paterson Street, a few blocks from where you got on, look to your left. Two immense metal birds tower over the bike path. The bird sculptures were created by local legend Dr. Evermor (aka Thomas O. Every), who makes incredibly expressive sculptures out of junk. His best-known creation, the Forevertron, weighs 400 tons and is docked in Baraboo, where Every lives and works.

These birds were made from a long laundry list of salvaged parts, including tubing from a semi that tipped over in Indiana. Their refreshing edginess is a perfect fit with the near east side sensibility.

From Paterson Street it's a short walk along the bike path and back to your car.

RESOURCES

- www.mononaterrace.com
  At Monona Terrace's website you'll find a lot of information about the building, its architect, parking, and other relevant information. You'll also see a magnificent photograph of the convention center at sunset.

- www.thirdlakeridge.org/data/photo_gallery.html
  Friends of Historic Third Lake Ridge has put up a wonderful series of historical photographs of Willy Street and surrounding blocks, taken over the last hundred years.

- www.velocitycomputing.com/madcity/page2.html
  Website of the Mad-City Ski Team, Madison's water-skiing show group.

- www.madfest.org
  Website of Madison Festivals, which sponsors Kites on Ice and other local celebrations.

- www.library.wisc.edu/etext/WIReader/WER0111.html
  This page from the Wisconsin Electronic Reader offers a fascinating sketch of Rosaline Peck and other Wisconsin pioneer women, written in 1924 by Florence Dexheimer, then state historian.

- danenet.wicip.org/hmi
  Website of Historic Madison, Inc., Madison's historical society, with links to information on publications, historic sites, images, and other elements.

- www.drevermor.org
  Dr. Evermor's own website.

13. Monona Bay
at Sunset

Perhaps the truth depends on a walk around the lake.
—Wallace Stevens

Proudfit and Brittingham

Natural interest, family friendly
Length: About 3 miles; 1 to 1-1/2 hours
Terrain: Flat; accessible to strollers and wheelchairs

Madison is famous for its four lakes: Mendota,
Monona, Wingra, and—what's the name of that fourth

lake? oh yes—Waubesa. Each of the lakes has reportedly been the site of a "large, unknown animal" sighting, along the lines of Nessie, the Loch Ness monster.

Mendota has the distinction of being the largest of the lakes. But Monona has something Mendota doesn't have: a bay, roughly 3 miles around, separated from the lake by a causeway. In winter the bay freezes well before the lake, making this a perfect spot for sighting large animals of a different sort—ice fishermen (and they're mostly men), in setups ranging from an overturned bucket to portable state-of-the-art ice-fishing shelters.

But you don't have to fish to enjoy the walk around Monona Bay at sunset, when the sun throws gorgeous colors onto the still waters of the bay, creating a fiery orange column, a shining beacon of light.

This walk is best begun about an hour and a half before sundown, so you get the full effect of nature's display. Park in the lot at Brittingham Park, at the corner of Proudfit and Brittingham Place; the public rest rooms in the shelter are reasonably clean and well maintained.

Walk toward the water on the lakeside path that follows Brittingham. This neighborhood, known as Bay Creek, is an appealing collection of modest, mostly unpretentious homes. It's the kind of neighborhood where you see a lot of American flags. A hundred years ago, it was an eclectic mix of German, Scandinavian, Russian, Irish, Bohemian, English, and Dutch, and it's still one of Madison's more diverse neighborhoods. Back then laborers walked to work downtown along the railroad bridges that cross Monona Bay. Nowadays there are big No Trespassing signs on all the bridges, so you have to take a slightly more circuitous route—but that's OK, because you're not in a hurry.

The No Trespassing signs don't stop the fisherfolk, though. On warm spring and summer days they're out in force along the railroad trestles—black and white, old and young, male and female, all of them looking for that tug on the line that promises dinner. A pole, a bucket, and a cooler is all you need to catch panfish, walleye, muskie, northern pike, largemouth bass, and other species in the waters of the bay.

This path is relatively new, and takes you through a lovely park. Not far away is a playground with swings, play equipment, and basketball hoops. Sit at a picnic table and let the kids play for a few minutes, enjoying the breeze from across the bay. Then keep moving. The path ends as you come around the corner onto West Shore, but the grassy verge along the water is actually public parkland. If you're pushing a stroller, you can always cross the street to the sidewalk.

People pay a premium to live on these few short
blocks by the bay, partly because of the fabulous view
of the capitol and downtown skyline, and partly
because they can put in private docks and boat
launches. Strolling by those docks is every bit as
satisfying as peeking into other people's living rooms.
There's a voyeuristic thrill to be had from admiring the
wrought-iron table and chairs on one dock (complete
with potted plant), the hammock on another, the blue
carpet and white plastic lawn furniture chained to the
third. Our favorite is lit at dusk with glowing lanterns
that look like small Japanese temples.

If you hear something thrashing in the otherwise still
water, stand still for a minute, and you may catch
sight of a carp. These muscular bottom feeders can
cause quite a splash as they root fiercely in the shallow
water near shore. The two-story birdhouses on poles
you see here and there are for purple martins, dark
swallows that live in colonies and are known for

eating quantities of insects—very useful in July, when the mosquitoes are at their peak.

Don't forget to cast a glance now and then at the houses across from the docks. Most are ordinary enough, but a few seem to subscribe to the code of individualism that pervades this neighborhood. Watch for the house with the butterfly bench and sea serpent, its stone coils rearing in fanciful loops from the pebbled surface of the yard.

Bernie's Beach, at the corner of Gilson, is an accessible sandy beach that's just the right size for little ones to swim and romp in the sand. It's a good place for a picnic, too, as long as you bring plenty of bug spray.

You could turn left and walk along the railroad tracks here, crossing the bay on trestles, but of course that would be illegal. So instead bear right onto Gilson, heading away from the bay. At Lakeside, a busy two-way street, turn left and walk past Lakeside Fibers, where you can buy yarn and supplies and take classes in knitting, weaving, and other fiber arts. Cross the railroad tracks and pass the Baha'i Center, spiritual home to the hundred or so local families who practice a faith based on the teachings of a nineteenth-century prophet named Bahá'u'lláh.

A block or two later you'll come to Franklin Elementary School, which serves students in kindergarten, first, and second grades from both the Bay Creek and University Heights neighborhoods. The Franklin playground gives kids yet another opportunity to run, swing, slide, and play.

Stay on Lakeside all the way to John Nolen Drive,
crossing at the traffic light. To your right is Olin-
Turville Park, another of Madison's terrific
neighborhood parks, with its own playground and
Lake Monona access. Turn left and follow the bike
path along the causeway. Lake Monona laps softly at
the tumbled rocks along its shoreline. To your left,
across John Nolen Drive, is Monona Bay. From this
angle you can see why some people think Monona
Terrace looks like a wedding cake.

At the end of the day, the setting sun is a burning
orange globe in the sky over the bay, throwing a
column of pure fire onto the still waters. The
occasional muskrat swims through the sunset, its
small brown head at the point of a "V," making steady
progress across the bay. Sit for a minute on a bench at
the public pier at the corner of North Shore, and
watch the fisherfolk cast for dinner.

To get back to the parking lot, cross John Nolen Drive
again and take the bike path beside the bay all the
way back.

RESOURCES
- www.ci.madison.wi.us/neighborhoods/profile/4.html
  Website of the Bay Creek Neighborhood Association.

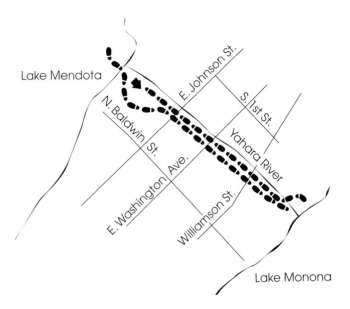

Lake Mendota

E. Johnson St.

S. 1st St.

N. Baldwin St.

Yahara River

E. Washington Ave.

Williamson St.

Lake Monona

14. Lake-to-Lake Walk

I have two doctors, my left leg and my right.
—G.M. Trevelyan

Thornton Avenue and Sherman Avenue

Natural interest, family friendly
Length: About 1.5 miles; 30 minutes to 1 hour
Loop: No
Terrain: Flat; trails range from paved to easy grass and
         dirt paths; accessible to strollers and
         wheelchairs

Madison may be home to four lakes, but most people
know only two of them: Mendota and Monona. This
short, easy walk takes you from one lake to the other
and back again.

Park in the lot at Thornton and Sherman and walk southeast along the Yahara River, which connects the lakes. Big signs prohibit duck feeding, but that doesn't faze the toddlers with bags full of bread. A paved drive follows the river through one end of Tenney Park. The drive curves right, but you go straight, veering away from the park itself. Follow the small paved path over the bridge that crosses the Tenney Park lagoon and cross East Johnson.

Now you're walking down the Yahara River Parkway, a grassy, parklike strip that parallels the Yahara River on your left and Thornton Street on your right, all the way to Lake Monona. In the nineteenth century, the area bordering the Yahara was a dumping ground for dead horses and garbage. Thanks to the efforts of Daniel Tenney and others at the turn of the last century, the river was widened and straightened to create a waterway between the lakes and the parkway was created. A series of graceful arching stone bridges (most of which are pedestrian walkways) crisscross the river, giving you plenty of opportunities for splendid views up and down the Yahara.

Rent a canoe at Carl's Paddlin (110 N. Thornton) and give your arms a workout, or keep hoofing your way along the grassy riverbank. You've got to hustle to get across busy East Washington Street; once you're across, look to your right for a stirring view of the capitol. Picnic benches appear here and there along the grassy verge, and tall reeds protect the riverbank from geese and other marauders, all courtesy of the Friends of the Yahara River Parkway.

Just before Main Street, veer left onto a small, pretty pebbled path that leads under another stone bridge and takes you to the water's edge. (This path is not recommended for strollers or wheelchairs.) Climb a steep staircase of stones up the bank; we've found some wonderful fossils in these stones. From the bridge, look southeast toward Lake Monona, taking in the sight of the serene and very well-managed riverbanks. Then continue southeast, crossing the railroad tracks and staying on the river side of the street.

On this section of the walk you'll pass several larches, also known as tamaracks. In fall their needles turn bright yellow and drop off, leading many people to think they're dying. But that's normal fall behavior for tamaracks, which are part of a curious family of trees known as deciduous conifers.

Cross Willy Street at Hans' Sewing and continue past locust and walnut trees twice the height of a person. If you're tired, sit for a moment on the bench at the corner of Jenifer Street, across from O'Keefe Middle School, and drink in the lovingly landscaped burst of flowers planted there. Then cross the river on the Jenifer Street bridge and, just for fun, look for the house with the bright pink door. This bank runs along Riverside Street, but it has the same grassy park and beautiful plantings as the bank along Thornton.

At Rutledge Street, follow the dirt path that heads southeast toward the lake. Two traffic lights—one red, one green—stand incongruously on either side of the river's outlet to Lake Monona. The lights guide boat traffic on the lake into the narrow Yahara, but they look as out of place as the lamppost in C.S. Lewis's Narnia.

Yahara Place Park begins at the confluence of lake and river, and stretches eastward to follow the lakeshore. You could keep going to the playground not far up the lakeshore. Or sit on the bench under the enormous cottonwood tree and admire the eccentric and appealing Chinese Fu Dog Lantern sculpture, created by local artist Sid Boyum, who died in 1991.

From here, make your way back to Tenney Park along the parkway, zigzagging across the bridges for a different perspective. Pass the parking lot and keep going toward Lake Mendota. With a little imagination and a gentle spring mist, you could be standing on the shore of Lake Michigan, the misty blues and grays of the water blending into the horizon.

Stroll out along the L-shaped jetty, which resembles an architect's rendering, all futuristic concrete and lampposts, benches, and boulders perfect for kids to adventure on. Then head for the only working lock in Madison. Due to what one writer has called a glacial practical joke, there's about a five-foot difference between the water levels of Lake Mendota and Lake Monona. So to get from one to another, boaters have to lock through Tenney Park, an activity that can take up to an hour on a busy summer afternoon.

The lock operates from May through October. With its mint-green tower and railings, it looks like a miniature pastel lighthouse. Spectating is a time-honored part of the locking process, so while away an hour or two listening to the instructions of the lock tender and watching the lock fill or drain to raise or lower boats.

From the lake, venture back across Sherman Avenue and into the park itself. In winter, people rent ice skates here or bring their own, gliding across the placid, shallow waters of the Tenney lagoon. In early July, people congregate to watch the city's annual Rhythm and Booms fireworks show.

The park has a
number of
graceful arched
stone bridges,
built in the late
1920s and early
1930s. Look for
a swamp white
oak with a small
stone marker
under it, honoring the memory of Marilyn
"Mimi" Orner, a much-loved feminist professor who
died in 2000.

Tenney Park is child friendly, with a playground and
basketball court. So find a bench, put up your feet,
and watch the kids swing, spin, dig, and dream.

RESOURCES

- designcoalition.org/comunity%20/boyum%20/boyum.htm
  See more of Sid Boyum's unusual public sculptures, many
  of which reside on Madison's East Side, including the Polar
  Bear Chair, the Smiling Mushroom, and the Fantasy
  Seahorse.

- www.madison.com/communities/cgaux/pages/article5.php?
  php_page_set=0
  Hints, tips, and information for navigating (and just
  admiring) the Tenney Locks.

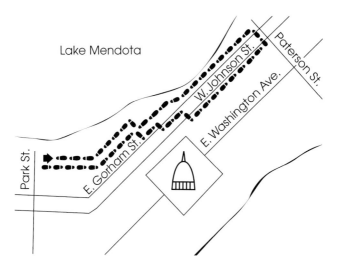

Lake Mendota

Park St.

E. Gorham St.

W. Johnson St.

E. Washington Ave.

Paterson St.

15. Memorial Union to Paterson Street

Everywhere is walking distance if you have the time.
—Steven Wright

Langdon Street and North Park Street

Family friendly, historical interest
Length: About 3.5 miles; 1 to 1-1/2 hours
Loop: Yes
Terrain: Easy pavement and city streets; accessible to
         wheelchairs and strollers

This walk is perfect for a Sunday morning. Even better
if you're visiting university students—it'll be hours
before they get up, plenty of time for you to explore

and experience some of the most interesting parts of
downtown Madison.

Start at Memorial Union, the heart and soul of the
campus, and head east on Langdon Street. Practically
right next door is an enormous red-brick Victorian
castle of a building. Its official name is the Armory
and Gymnasium, but everyone calls it the Red Gym.
Whatever you call it, it's hard to take your eyes off it.

Built in 1893, the Red Gym was the site of many
famous (and infamous) town-and-gown events,
including the contentious Republican state political
convention of 1904, the first performance of "On
Wisconsin" in 1909, and assorted proms and
basketball games. By the 1950s the building was in
disrepair. Named a historic landmark in 1994, it was
rebuilt and reopened to great fanfare in 1998, and
now houses the university's student and visitor
services center.

Ignore its prosaic present, and take in the building's
fantasy castle element, from the crenellated turrets and
vertical arrow loops to the great medieval-looking
doors, their arched silhouettes traced with metalwork.

Next door is the Pyle Center, a University of
Wisconsin–Extension distance learning and conference
center. Its boxy cream-colored walls and glass
outlooks seem disconcertingly modern beside the Red
Gym. Make a left onto Lake Street and find a little
concrete pier perfect for taking photographs against
the backdrop of Lake Mendota.

Continue along Langdon Street. In the mid-nineteenth century, Langdon was a long way from Madison's tiny downtown—too long for people to actually live there. In 1851 a few intrepid and wealthy Madisonians built mansions along this street, and the rest, as they say, is history. By the turn of the century, there were 3,000 students at the University of Wisconsin, and a suitable number of faculty who needed places to live. Thus Langdon Street became a popular address.

Today this stretch of Langdon is filled with apartments and student housing. One of these is the Roundhouse (626), a modern apartment tower with rows of balconies climbing some of its 12 sides. Across the street is the university's Hillel Foundation, which sponsors Israeli dancing, coffeehouses, classes in kashrut, and many other Jewish-themed activities. Turn left on North Frances Street and make your way down the block to 629 for a glimpse of the modest house where historian Frederick Jackson Turner lived at the height of his career.

The next few blocks of Langdon are packed with fraternities and sororities, in buildings that range from the historic to the thoroughly modern, from the seedy to the stately. There are beautiful brick buildings festooned with ivy, and rundown houses with sagging porches and splatters of student garbage. Practice your knowledge of the Greek alphabet by reading their names, proudly emblazoned on the front of each building in three-foot-high Greek letters. Look for the words "Fight Sexism" etched in the concrete outside of one of them.

Turn left on Henry for a close-up of Madison's ubiquitous purple houses. (See the box on page 119.) There must be half a dozen or more of these scattered around town, but Rivendell Co-op (622) wins the prize for best and brightest. This housing co-op—one of about a dozen in Madison—has been going strong for more than 25 years.

Continue down Henry to the end of the street, where a set of stairs leads you to a little grassy area at the lakeshore. In summer you're likely to see student debris—an old boot, beer cups, soda cans, and yes, used prophylactics. But the view of the lake is peaceful and pretty. Winter is more scenic; the snow covers most of the debris, and once the lake freezes

over you can often find groups of students playing baseball out on the ice.

Head back up to Langdon, past herds of scooters parked outside houses and apartments—a favored mode of transportation for cash-strapped students. Turn left and continue east, past private residence halls and more fraternities. Langdon Street ends at Wisconsin Avenue, site of the Edgewater Hotel (one of Madison's classiest places to stay), but you can cross Wisconsin Avenue and follow the sidewalk away from the lake.

Turn left when you reach Gilman Street. The Keenan House (28 E. Gilman) was designed in 1857, in a style one guidebook describes as "German Romanesque revival." Whatever it's called, this faux castle has entryway posts shaped like chess rooks and a Victorian gingerbread topping good enough to eat.

Across the street at 424 N. Pinckney Street is the McDonnell/Pierce House, now the Mansion Hill Inn, a Romanesque revival house built in 1858. Even if you know (or care) little about architecture, you can't help but admire its arched windows, filigreed balcony railings and columns, and the creamy Prairie du Chien sandstone blocks it's built from.

Continue east on
Gilman, past the
Knapp House (130),
an Italianate-style
sandstone building
that was home to 17
Wisconsin governors
between 1885 and
1950, and which
now belongs to the
university. The
Gilman Street Rag, a
bed and breakfast

(125), is one of a number of beautiful examples of
refurbished late Victorians, complete with wraparound
porch, tower, and copper roofing.

Gilman Street ends at North Butler, but the walk
continues. Follow the concrete path to the right,
around to the left, and past a small blacktop and
basketball hoop. Turn right and stroll by Gates of
Heaven, a boxy Italianate beauty of a building
designed by August Kutzbock (who designed Keenan
House, the McDonnell/Pierce House, and many of the
buildings in this part of town).

Gates of Heaven was Madison's first synagogue, built
on West Washington Avenue for a congregation of
German Jewish immigrants in 1863. Throughout the
first three-quarters of the twentieth century the
building took on various identities, including funeral
parlor, government storage facility, headquarters of the
Women's Christian Temperance Union, and veterinary
clinic. After it was slated for demolition in 1970 (to

make room for a new office building), a group of Madisonians raised enough money to have the building put on the National Register of Historic Places, and eventually jacked up onto 96 aircraft wheels and rolled through a mile of downtown Madison to its current home. The city owns it now, making it available to groups ranging from contra dancers to Sufi worshipers to private wedding parties. Two days a year, Gates of Heaven is still a synagogue, hosting Rosh Hashanah and Yom Kippur services open to all.

Continue east into the rest of James Madison Park. The park hugs the Lake Mendota shoreline, making it a prime sunset-watching spot. During the school year, this park is a student hangout, full of dogs, bandannas, and flying Frisbees. In the early morning, sculls ply the waters of the lake, and joggers and walkers wind along a path by the shore. Let the children burn off energy on the playground; there are strategically placed benches for exhausted parents. Or rent a canoe or kayak at the shelter at the far end of the park and paddle around for a while.

When you're ready to move on, follow the lakeshore path east to a set of stairs that climbs to Gorham Street. There's a lovely little garden planted at the top of the stairs, and a pleasing view of Lake Mendota. Continue east on Gorham, through a part of town that has been known through the years as Big Bug Hill, Yankee Hill, Aristocrat Hill, and now Mansion Hill.

As all of these names suggest, this was one of
Madison's most prestigious neighborhoods in the latter
half of the nineteenth century, home to bankers,
timber barons, railroad lawyers, real estate promoters,
university professors, and judges. You can still see
some of the spectacular houses built here 150 years
ago, though few are still single-family homes. One of
our favorites is Leitch House (752 E. Gorham), a
Gothic revival made from sandstone brought across
Fourth Lake (now Lake Mendota) on barges. It was
built for William Leitch, a New York clothier who was
mayor of Madison for three terms running.

Turn right at Paterson Street and go one block south
to East Johnson. Read the sign on the Norris Court
Grocery, and then head across Johnson Street to
Burnie's Rock Shop for gems and lapidary treasures.
Turn right onto East Johnson, heading west for the
return leg of this loop. This block is something of a
haven for artists, with many browsable galleries and
shops. The Wendy Cooper Gallery (824 E. Johnson) is
one of Madison's best respected galleries, showing
both regional and national work by painters,
photographers, and other visual artists. Sophia's

Bakery and Café (831), a funky little neighborhood café, serves some of the best pastries west of New York City's Veniero's.

If you like embroidery, crewelwork, and other needle arts, stop in at Florilegium (821). And check out the wild door decorations at Aardvark Art Glass (819)—they're reminiscent of the kind of graffiti Keith Haring painted in the New York City subways in the early 1980s.

One of our personal favorites in this neighborhood is Jade Mountain Bead and Jewelry (817), a small shop bursting with every kind of bead imaginable. Work your way through the store, admiring a rainbow of glass, crystal, ceramic, wooden, and metal beads hanging in long strings from hooks. Jade Mountain sells every kind of beading accessory and offers classes. Down the block, the cool art supplies at Artist and Craftsman Supply (811) will make you wish you were an artist. We always stock up here on blank cards and colorful vellum envelopes.

Continue west along East Johnson, past another, paler purple building at 649 and lots of idiosyncratic student housing. Turn right at the five-way intersection of Johnson, Butler, and Hamilton, and then take another left and head uphill on Gorham. In the mid-nineteenth century, Keyes House (102 E. Gorham) was owned by Elizabeth and Elisha Keyes. Elisha Keyes was a powerful Republican boss who became a symbol of political corruption for "Fighting Bob" La Follette, one of Wisconsin's leading Progressive politicians. Keyes House is now

apartments, but its front yard has been preserved as
an elegant garden by local residents.

Turn right on Pinckney and left again onto East
Gilman. At the corner of Gilman and Wisconsin look
to your left. There's the Wisconsin State Capitol in all
its gleaming white glory, looking like the White
House. The gold-leafed statue on top of the capitol
dome was created by sculptor Daniel French.

Retrace your earlier steps until you're back on
Langdon Street. The Alpha Phi sorority (28) was once
home to Frank Brown, who helped found Rayovac.
Follow Langdon back to Memorial Union, where you
can take a waffle cone full of Babcock Hall ice cream
out onto the Terrace, find a chair, and feel virtuous for
the rest of the day.

RESOURCES

- In the 1980s, Madison Heritage published a wonderful
  series of booklets, each about 30 pages, on the architecture
  and history of some of Madison's historic neighborhoods,
  including *Madison's Pioneer Buildings: A Downtown
  Walking Tour* (Madison Landmarks Commission and
  Historic Madison, Inc., 1987), *The Langdon Street Historic
  District: A Walking Tour* (City of Madison, 1986), and
  The First Settlement Neighborhood: A Walking Tour
  (Madison Landmarks Commission and Capitol
  Neighborhoods, 1988).

Where Are All the Purple Houses?

How many purple houses are there in Madison? We counted four: Rivendell Co-op on North Henry, the apartment building at 649 E. Johnson, and both 1415 and 1435–37 Williamson Street. How many do you know about? Send your count of lavender, fuchsia, magenta, and plain purple houses to us at hnbrown@tds.net, and we may post them on the Jones Books website at www.jonesbooks.com.

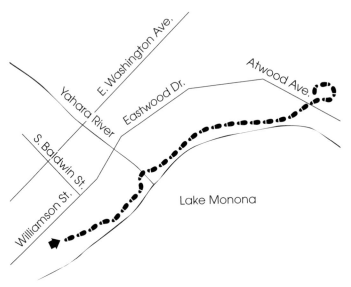

16. Orton Park to Olbrich Gardens

A vigorous five-mile walk will do more good for an unhappy but otherwise healthy adult than all the medicine and psychology in the world.—Paul Dudley White

Spaight Street and Ingersoll Street

Family friendly, natural interest
Length: 3.5 miles; 1 to 1-1/2 hours (plus whatever time you spend at Olbrich Gardens)
Loop: No
Terrain: Easy pavement; accessible to wheelchairs and strollers

This easy jaunt through city streets takes you past three playgrounds, three public sculptures, a treasure of a botanical garden, and the only open-air Thai *sala,* or pavilion, in North America.

Begin at the northwest edge of Orton Park, at the corner of Spaight and Ingersoll streets. This near east side neighborhood is full of big Victorian homes in various states of repair. The Curtis-Kittleson House (102 Spaight) is a redbrick Queen Anne beauty, with burnt orange cornices and the kind of tower every kid dreams of living in. Like so many of the historic homes in and around Madison, this one was home to one of the city's mayors—William Curtis, who held that office from 1904 to 1906.

Take the paved path that leads diagonally through Orton Park, Madison's first public park. In the mid-1840s, this square of land was the cemetery for the fledgling village of Madison, but by the late 1880s the bodies buried here had been disinterred and reburied in the new cemetery at Forest Hill. In 1887, Harlow S. Orton, a Wisconsin Supreme Court justice and dean of the university law school, cast the deciding vote that turned this land into a park. His reward was in the naming.

Orton Park has a pair of basketball hoops and a playground. The park's tall oaks and hickories give it a leafy, breezy feeling even in the dog days of summer. Leave the park at its southeast corner and continue east on Rutledge Street, through a funky and never boring neighborhood where you're likely to see dreadlocks, prairie flowers, and cell phones within a block of one another. Many of the Victorian houses in this neighborhood have eye-popping trim in

bright pink, blue, or purple that belies their aura of staid history.

Turn right on Baldwin for one block and make a left onto Morrison Court. The houses along this street are newer; many look like they date from the 1950s and '60s. The houses on the south side of the street have backyards right on the lake, many of which include private docks and boats.

At Dickinson go right a short block to a bench, strategically placed on the lakeshore. Then continue down Rutledge, passing tiny Morrison Park with its small play structure, swings, and picnic table. Morrison Court dead-ends at the outlet of the Yahara River (and crosses walk #14, the Lake-to-Lake Walk; see page 106). Dogleg back up to Rutledge to the car and pedestrian bridge that makes this a major thoroughfare. From the bridge you can watch stinkpots (one of the many uncomplimentary names given to motorboats by those who sail) slowly move up the Yahara, heading toward Lake Mendota.

Make a right on Riverside, on the other bank, and follow the dirt path down to Yahara Place Park. Pass the Chinese Fu Dog Lantern sculpture and head east along the park, a wide grassy strip that hugs the shoreline. This park boasts a horseshoe court, a volleyball net, a number of picnic tables, and a playground half-shaded by enormous cottonwoods and lindens. If you're fairly immune to mosquitoes (or have plenty of bug spray on), take the narrow dirt path that runs close to the water and enjoy the views across Lake Monona.

If you're doing this walk in spring or summer, you will no doubt notice the infamous "lake smell," which conjures unpleasant visions of decaying fish. For all their beauty, Madison's lakes face the same problems as other urban watersheds, including algae, weeds, and pollution, and many people refuse to swim in them.

The park comes to an end at Dunning Street. Go left one block to Lakeland and turn right. You can stay on this grassy lakeside verge all the way to Olbrich Park. A couple of blocks up, follow the dirt path through Hudson Park. This park and the next one you'll come to, Elmside, were created in the early 1900s to preserve a series of effigy mounds. The mound in Hudson Park is believed to depict a panther or water spirit.

Follow the dirt path a few blocks to the crest of the hill, where you can rest on a bench in Elmside Park near "Let the Great Spirits Soar," a 13-foot sculpture carved from a single hackberry tree that had been struck by lightning. Local artist Harry Whitehorse created it as a testament to his Ho-Chunk ancestors and to the mound builders. People arrange offerings on the concrete base of the sculpture—beads, votives, a stone painted with petroglyphs.

Across from the sculpture on Lakeland is the Riley House, the first house erected in Madison by local architect Frank M. Riley. He built this house in 1908 for his parents, and it's now a landmark.

From here, Lakeland heads downhill. Cut over on a paved drive to the right and into Olbrich Park, where you'll pass the second sculpture on this walk. This one comprises three upright panels, each with mysterious lines carved onto them. When you stand in just the right spot, the three panels converge and a trick of the eye creates an image of a person resting on one elbow. The panels are carved from both sides, and the same illusion is created on the back.

The park has public bathrooms, picnic tables, a charcoal grill, and a good playground, all on the way

to sculpture number three, an imposing silver construction depicting four sticklike figures towering 25 feet over the ground. A short, grassy pier juts out into Lake Monona, where you can watch the jet skiers, stinkpots, and sailboats, or put in a boat of your own. The park was named for Michael Olbrich, an attorney and university regent who spent years raising the money for the park and then sold it to the city of Madison at no profit to himself. Olbrich died in 1929 at the age of 48, but his vision lives on, in both the park and Olbrich Gardens.

To get to the gardens you have to cross busy Atwood Avenue, without benefit of crosswalk or traffic light. It's worth it, though. This wonderful botanical garden complex comprises 10 outdoor "specialty" gardens (including a sunken garden and a spectacular rock garden) and the Bolz Tropical Conservatory, an indoor glass-domed conservatory that contains many of the flora and fauna found in a tropical rainforest, including banana leaves as big as your head, blue-faced parrot finches, giant golden koi, geckos, coffee trees, and many other exotic species. The conservatory is a popular destination during Madison's long, cold winters, when a stroll through an overheated tropical rainforest is a lot cheaper than a Caribbean vacation.

The outdoor gardens are popular, too; on summer afternoons it's common to see serial wedding parties posing in the Olin Fountain Perennial Garden. Follow the paths that weave through all the outdoor gardens to find a series of exquisite themed plantings—roses of every imaginable color, extravagant hostas, creeping mosses, towering grasses, and more, all of it sprung up in the last 25 years, a legacy of Michael Olbrich's original gift.

The latest jewel in Olbrich's crown is the Thai Pavilion and Garden, at the northern edge of the gardens. To reach it, cross Starkweather Creek on an intricately decorated bridge and step into a lush garden where stone elephants nestle beside angel's trumpet, princess trees, umbrella magnolia, and other tropical plantings, some of which are dug up and brought inside each winter and then replanted each spring. The bridge and winding path symbolize a great naga, or serpent, a traditional Thai figure representing the power of rain, wind, and thunderstorms. "The idea is to make people feel that when they've crossed that bridge, they've stepped into Thailand," explains Jeff Epping, Olbrich's horticulture director. We've never actually been to Thailand, but we imagine it just like this.

The head of the naga is the gleaming golden Thai Pavilion, which sits serenely before a reflecting pool. The 40-foot-long open-air sala is an effulgence of red and gold, covered with intricate gold leaf etching and crowned with a delicately peaked golden roof. Its sinuous carvings are lacquered to a shiny finish, giving the pavilion the look of a glowing golden jewel.

In Thailand, simple salas are used as street shelters from heat and rain, but this is no ordinary shelter. This $2 million pavilion commemorates the 72nd birthday of the king of Thailand. It's a gift from the Thai chapter of the University of Wisconsin Alumni Association to the university, which reportedly has one of the largest Thai student populations of any U.S. university. The pavilion was built in Thailand entirely by hand, taken apart, and then re-assembled on-site (using no nails or joinery) by a team of Thai artisans over a period of six weeks.

When you're ready to head back to the real world, retrace your steps all the way to Orton Park.

RESOURCES

- www.wisconsinstories.org/2001season/native/nj_journey.html
  Information on some of Wisconsin's effigy mounds, both lost and preserved.

- www.harrywhitehorse.com
  A virtual gallery tour of Harry Whitehorse's sculptures, with information about the artist and his work.

- www.madison.com/captimes/thai
  Take a virtual tour of the Thai pavilion at Olbrich Gardens here.

- www.olbrich.org
  Website for Olbrich Gardens.

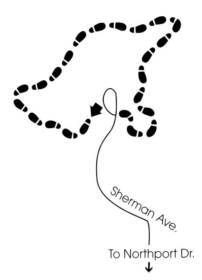

Sherman Ave.

To Northport Dr.
↓

17. Cherokee Marsh

*In every walk with nature one receives far more
than he seeks.*—John Muir

Off Sherman Avenue

Natural interest
Length: About 1.5 miles; 30 minutes to 1-1/2 hours
Loop: Yes
Terrain: Mostly flat; not recommended for strollers and
              wheelchairs

If you enjoy the varieties of flora, fauna, and vista
contained in marshy areas, you'll enjoy a stroll
through Cherokee Marsh. The marsh contains
several types of wetland communities, including fen,

wet prairie, and sedge meadow; and while you will likely meet other hikers along your way, the overall feeling and experience of this walk is peaceful, isolated, and serene.

From the parking lot take the grassy trail leading to the left. Bear right at the first fork and head away from the parking lot, onto a dirt trail. The trail heads slightly uphill, with woods to the right and prairie to the left. Walk this way in April or May and you'll hear the famous spring peepers, *Pseudacris crucifer crucifer,* small frogs whose mating calls are a familiar herald of spring all over Wisconsin. Holden Caulfield wondered where all the fish and ducks from Central Park go in the winter; maybe he should have asked about spring peepers. These little frogs actually freeze over the long Wisconsin winters, but their cells stay intact because of naturally high levels of concentrated sugars. (Or, as one website puts it, "These sugars act as a kind of natural anti-freeze.") Pretty good adaptation.

The trail leads to a dirt service drive. Turn left onto the drive and take the first trail leading to the right. This is an easy walk through swampland studded with big willows and bright with birdsong. About 150 yards down the trail, you catch a glimpse of water, wide and sparkling, a shining blue scarf over the lip of the land.

The trail passes the Conical Mound, an early cone-shaped mound (as the name suggests). Stand beside the mound and just look. Except for the sign next to the mound and the trail, everything you see might

have been here 2,000 years ago, when the mound builders lived, worked, played, and died here. That's how it struck us on a spring afternoon—at least until the thunder of a pair of F-16s made the trees shake.

Continue downhill to the water. The only signs of human habitation are a couple of houses across the lake. From here you can meander down a weathered gray boardwalk that snakes along the shore, part of the Cherokee Wetland Restoration Project. The project is part of an ongoing effort to repair the damage caused to the wetland by the installation of a sewer pipe in the 1970s.

Sewer pipes notwithstanding, this is a beautiful, serene place to walk, quiet except for the trilling of birdsong. Climb the steps to the observation platform for a gorgeous view of marshland and woods. This is a view you can't find anywhere else in Madison, a combination of wide, flat water, blond prairie grasses waving, fish jumping out on the water, and red-winged blackbirds flashing by.

The boardwalk continues on a few yards, depositing you onto another wide dirt trail. Turn left onto the trail and then branch almost immediately off to the right, onto a small side trail that leads uphill. Patches of white flowers and pale lavender greeted us here one spring afternoon.

As it climbs the hill, the path winds through cherry trees, shagbark hickories, and oak. At the very top there's a bench, so you can pause to admire the view: a 200-degrees-plus panorama encompassing Token Creek in the distance, a wide expanse of glacial moraine, and a stretch of Interstate 90 glinting near the horizon.

When you've had your fill of visual splendor, take the mowed grassy trail to the right, down the shoulder of the hill. (The children among you will want to roll down at least part of this gentle slope.) Dragonflies skim the tops of the dried grasses. At the bottom of the hill you can turn right and go back to the parking lot along the wide path, or, if you're feeling hardy, cross it and head downhill again.

This path is much rougher than the rest of the walk, with water-filled potholes and bumpy terrain riddled with channels of water. Be prepared for a lot of up, down, and squish. The trail curves to the right, giving you a glimpse of another observation platform to your left. After a short distance it emerges triumphantly from the swampy area, and you're back on dry land. Turn left onto a short boardwalk that loops quickly back to the trail, and then take a second boardwalk to the left to reach the observation platform you saw a little ways back.

If you've had enough squish for one day, turn
right and take the mowed path through a section of
prairie. Watch for flashes of gold skimming the tall
grasses—goldfinches noisily going about their
business. Our seven-year-old was enchanted with
them one spring afternoon. "It sounds like they're
saying, 'Come and play with me! Come and play!'"
she reported. And it did.

The mowed path takes you back to the parking
lot, where with any luck you've got a pair of dry
shoes stashed in the car. You'll probably need them
about now.

RESOURCES

- For information on spring peepers and other
  Wisconsin frogs, see www.dnr.state.wi.us/org/caer/ce/eek/
  critter/amphibian/frogident.htm.

- For information on the Cherokee Wetland Restoration
  Project, call 608-267-4918.

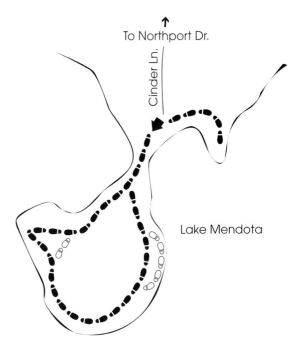

To Northport Dr.

Cinder Ln.

Lake Mendota

18. Governor's Island

If you are seeking creative ideas, go out walking.
Angels whisper to a man when he goes for a walk.
—Raymond Inmon

Off Cinder Lane

Natural interest

Length: Between 1 and 2 miles, depending on how many side trails you explore; 30 minutes to 1 hour

Loop: Yes

Terrain: Dirt paths, slightly rough terrain; not recommended for wheelchairs and strollers

Note: Wear a hat, as this trail is very buggy in late spring and summer

This short jaunt is ideal for introducing kids to the everyday natural world, or for a Sunday stroll with a good friend. It's a pleasant little walk, combining bird-watching and a sense of natural serenity with history.

The history part comes largely on the way to Governor's Island, because you can get there only by driving through the Mendota Mental Health Institute, a state psychiatric hospital on Madison's north side. Driving through the grounds always reminds us of a Merchant-Ivory film. The large, spread-out buildings, the rolling green lawns, the feeling of containment conjure a sense of gentility usually associated with England between the wars. You wouldn't be at all surprised to see men in plus fours playing croquet and women in white trailing dresses carrying parasols, idling in the sun.

On the way, see if you can spot the eagle effigy mound on Mendota's grounds. With a wingspan of 624 feet, it's reputed to be the largest eagle mound in the world. We believe it. According to Mendota's website, this eagle mound, along with turtle and deer mounds also on the grounds, are aligned to correspond with the North Star, moon, and sun, respectively.

Mendota is located near the community of Maple Bluff, one of Madison's toniest places to live. The governor's house is here, as are the houses of many of Madison's upper crust. Maple Bluff has always been an upscale neighborhood. In the 1880s, well-heeled

Madisonians built summer "cottages" here. The Maple Bluff Golf Club, founded circa 1899, was the first golf course in Madison. Mendota Mental Health dates from the same era; it opened its doors in the 1860s as an "asylum for the insane," and has been in constant use ever since. It's interesting that two such diverse, self-contained communities have existed cheek by jowl for more than a hundred years.

Governor's Island is actually a small, teardrop-shaped peninsula that extends into Lake Mendota. (Why is it called an island? We couldn't find out.) From Mendota's Main Drive, turn left onto Cinder Lane and follow it a short way to the Governor's Island parking lot. A trail leads from the parking lot onto the peninsula, through a wooded area where you'll see enormous willow trees with gray ridged bark. Bear right at a fork in the path and continue on, listening for birdsong and enjoying the pastoral scenery.

To your right is a little bay, where motorboats like to anchor for rest and relaxation in the sun. The path is a little rough, and you'll have to step over some big roots and stumps. Watch for jewelweed by the side of the trail. This common little plant with its softly serrated leaves and jewel-like orange or yellow flowers is an excellent antidote to the ubiquitous mosquitoes; crush a leaf and rub it on a fresh bite for quick relief.

Bear right onto a sandy trail that goes right to the water, winding along a narrow strip of land. Listen for the sound of the waves lapping at the sandy shore. After a little while you'll pass a small metal shack painted with graffiti, including the message "Blessed are the sick." You may have to duck and weave your way through the overgrown scrub here, but it's worth it. You come out onto a small point with a scumble of gray boulders—a good place to sit in full sun and listen to the music blasting from the motorboats in the bay.

Go back the way you came to the trail and continue on to the right, watching for plants that look like bamboo by the side of the path. This main path is a big loop, with side trails leading off in every direction. You can stay on the main path and keep your walk short and easy, or take the time to explore some of the smaller trails. A number of small bumpy paths run along the top of a bank with a drop-off to the water. It's an easy slide down the short, steep slope to stand on a sandy outcrop in the sun, where you can look across the lake at Picnic Point and the capitol.

If you follow the shoreline, you'll find yourself on a small bluff above the water, where a dirt path leads through knee-high grass and woods laced with berry bushes and Solomon's seal. From some vantage points you can look across at the greenswards and mansions of Maple Bluff. After a while the side path leaves the water and heads into a dense section of woods, and shortly thereafter it ends in a T. Turn left, away from the water, and join back up with the main path.

When the main path forks, take either branch; they come together again 20 feet down the trail. Continue along the path to the parking lot. If you're up for a little more walking, find a roadway at the other end of the parking lot (not the one you came in on) and turn right. Pass a swath of coarse sawgrass, and bear right before the sign reading "Off limits beyond this point." Now you're curving up along the other bank of one of the small bays surrounding Governor's Island, past a number of impressive weeping willows. At the end of this small bump of land is a marvelous view of the lake, including the capitol, parts of the university, and Maple Bluff. (Judging by the scattered beer cans and cigarette butts on the ground, this is a popular hangout at night.)

A small ring of stones extends into the water. If you're feeling particularly nimble (and don't mind the possibility of getting wet), you can step from stone to stone, walking out onto the lake. Or sit on a stone on a hot summer's day and dangle your feet into the cool water, and head back to the car when you're ready.

RESOURCES

- www.villageofmaplebluff.com/history.html
  Information on the history of Maple Bluff, from volume 12 of *Historic Madison: A Journal of the Four Lake Region* (Historic Madison, Inc., 1995).

- www.dhfs.state.wi.us/MH_Mendota/Mendota/MMHIHist.htm
  This section of the website for the Mendota Mental Health Institute has interesting information about effigy mounds.

Index